BACK TO WORK

BACK TO WORK

Determinants of Women's
Successful Re-entry

EILEEN APPELBAUM
Temple University

Auburn House Publishing Company
Boston, Massachusetts

This book is based on a report prepared for the Employment and Training Administration, U.S. Department of Labor, under research and development grant No. 21-42-78-51. The statements, findings, conclusions, and recommendations herein do not necessarily represent the official opinion or policy of the Department of Labor.

Library of Congress Cataloging in Publication Data
Appelbaum, Eileen, 1940–
    Back to work.

    Includes index.
    1. Women—Employment—United States—Longitudinal studies.   I. Title.
HD6095.A69   331.4'0973   81-8008
ISBN 0-86569-076-6   AACR2

Printed in the United States of America

FOREWORD

We hear so much about the social revolution in women's work attachment that we tend to forget that the rising labor force participation rates measured at one point in time include rates for women with a variety of work patterns over time. For some, attachment is full time, permanent, and continuous. For others, attachment may be continuous but part time or part year. For still other women, full-time or part-time work may be interspersed with periods of withdrawal from the labor market while they are involved in non-market productive activities relating to home and family.

Data of recent years reflect this diversity of life cycle work patterns rather than movement of a homogeneous group of homemakers to a group composed solely of continuous, full-time paid workers from age 21 to retirement. It is true, for example, that full-time year-round women workers are increasing as a proportion of all groups, whether the comparison be by age, marital status, or presence and ages of children. But many of the growing numbers of working women are choosing to work part time. Between May 1968 and May 1977, women accounted for about four fifths of the growth of 2.5 million voluntary part-time workers. Although they currently constitute 43 percent of all civilian workers, they represent more than one half of all voluntary, non-agricultural part-time workers.[1] Moreover, the variation in the degree of permanence of women's labor force attachment is reflected in a study of working wives between 1968 and 1977 which reported that, although 82 percent of these women had earning of $100 or more in at least one year out of ten, only 21 percent had such earnings in all ten years. Only 44 percent of the married women could be called permanent members of the labor force, defined as having these minimum earnings in at least seven out of the ten years.[2]

What these work rhythms suggest is that although paid work has become an integral part of the lives of a majority of women, family demands—demands which they respond to in different ways in different phases and circumstances of their lives—compete for the use of their time. Despite the increased variability of family forms over the individual life span, the conventional marriage continues to predominate. And although family size is smaller today and having children is postponed to a later age than ten years ago, children are not disappearing as a part of our lives. Their care as well as the pleasure of their company requires both time and energy. The need to mesh demands of family and work will continue, whether the responsibility is carried largely by women, as now, or is shared in a more symmetrical family relationship.

It is for these reasons that Eileen Appelbaum's book, far from being an historical study of a cohort whose experience is fast becoming irrelevant, is of tremendous importance for both women and men today. The competing demands of work and family life can be partially met (or avoided) by reducing the size of families, and to some degree they are. They can be coped with by a greater sharing of home-related tasks by men and women. Some, though not a great deal, of this kind of change in gender roles has been recorded. When it occurs, it is more likely to relate to child care tasks than to housekeeping duties. But much of the required adaptation still centers around alterations in work. Discontinuities in paid work, most evident in the work patterns of wives, continue to be an important coping mechanism today, as they have been in the past, for meeting family needs.

It is with these paid work discontinuities—their timing and their consequences—that Dr. Appelbaum's study is concerned. Following an overview chapter that discusses the rise of the working wife and mother and the low earnings she has traditionally received, the book undertakes a meticulous comparative empirical analysis of costs and other consequences of work intermittency. It focuses on two groups of white women, ages 30–44, who were members of the National Longitudinal Survey sample of 5,000 women representing the 18 million women in the U.S. noninstitutional civilian population in 1967, and traces their experience through seven personal, mail, and telephone interviews through 1977. The first group left the labor force following marriage or birth of a first child and did not return to paid employment for at least three years. The average length of absence from paid work was 11.7 years. The second sample was of women who were absent from the labor force for less than three years. What is compared, then, is the differing experience of women who have had extended paid work discontinuities, and those whose time away from paid work was of much shorter duration. It is as rare as it is important to have available analysis of longitudinal data based on real world experience for assessing alternative patterns of labor market experience and for formulating recommendations for institutional and policy improvements.

Does the length of the paid work break matter? Indeed it does. Dr. Appelbaum demonstrates that the economic costs of an extended break are greater than for a shorter break in hourly earnings received, in increased earnings over time after return to work, and in prestige status (Chapter 3). For women with extended breaks, the husband's approval is an important factor in job satisfaction; hourly earnings and social status on the job, but not husband's approval, are the explanatory variables that significantly affect job satisfaction of women with shorter breaks in paid work (Chapter 4). The ability to make a successful re-entry is enhanced by years of schooling (although not by the kind of schooling), by choice of college major, by participation in post-school training programs, and by the characteristics of jobs held early in the career (Chapter 5).

By way of contrast to these effects of work withdrawal, Chapter 6 analyzes the characteristics and consequences of part-time jobs, an alternative way in which work pressures can be reduced while avoiding the negative earnings and status consequences associated with a break in work attachment. Unfortunately, part-time work has negative consequences of its own. Both author and reader must conclude from the data presented that in its present form part-time work is no panacea for resolving the dilemma of competing work/family demands. But what if the concept were to be enlarged? What if it applied to a broader occupational range and was thoughtfully developed to include jobs of greater skill and responsibility? What if fringe benefits, especially pro-rated pension and health benefits, were included in part-time compensation? What if career progression were possible for part-time as well as for full-time work? Could not part-time work then offer more than an opportunity for low earnings, often intermittent, at low-level jobs? Could not such part-time work become a more appropriate vehicle for maintaining continuity of work attachment, so critical not only for retaining skills but also for building credits for later social security benefits? It seems to me that skill retention could result both in a higher level of earnings and in a greater growth rate commensurate with increased experience. Creative thinking about this issue could transform this work structure and its life-cycle benefits, not only to relieve the strain of technological unemployment or provide supplementary retirement income but also to benefit all by not wasting the skills and work experience of societal members who want to work.

Although not optimistic about a continuation in the future of the growth rate of women's work opportunities, Dr. Appelbaum perceives their continued interest in working, an interest fostered by economic necessity and a desire to maintain the family standard of living. In her study she does more than hold up a mirror so that we may see clearly the consequences of short-term and extended labor force withdrawals. She offers guidelines for individual decision making by highlighting the earnings benefits that accrue to training and education and ensuring that strong educational and prestige characteristics adhere to the jobs held early in the career. Moreover, she supports the introduction of social policies to foster improvements in labor market structures, increased employment opportunities, and improved quality of jobs available to women. These will necessitate new government policies such as those that eliminate disincentives to employers caused by higher employer social security taxes for two part-time workers as against one worker of equivalent wage. And they will require identification and removal of exogenous constraints on working hours, such as the lack of day care.

It is time that the social revolution of women's engagement in paid work be matched by a parallel movement of institutional and policy adaptation to facilitate a balance between work and family activities. Dr. Appelbaum has provided evidence that highlights the dramatic lack of responsiveness of work rhythms to family needs to date and the negative consequences that flow when extended paid work discontinuities result. But she also directs our attention to possible adjustments of work structures, institutional policies, and reward systems that will better respond to the rhythms of our contemporary lives. If thoughtfully constructed, these new modes of living need not be in contradiction to the traditional goals of the marketplace. In fact, as some enterprises in the private sector are beginning to suggest, such quality of work life improvements may even be reflected in an increase in productivity—one sought-after result by which success of innovative change is measured.

HILDA KAHNE
WHEATON COLLEGE

Endnotes

1. Derived from data in Deutermann, William V. Jr., and Scott Campbell Brown, "Voluntary Part-time Workers: A Growing Part of the Labor Force," *Monthly Labor Review*, Vol. 10, No. 6, June 1978, p. 5.
2. Masnick, George, and Mary Jo Bane, *The Nation's Families: 1960–1990* (Boston: Auburn House Publishing Company, 1980), p. 71.

PREFACE

Women and work have been the subject of much public discussion as sociologists, economists, and social commentators try to explain the dramatic increase in paid employment of married women and evaluate the consequences of this change. Most affected by the shifting events and the new patterns of social interaction that conditioned the changes in both women's work and in the place of women within the family was the cohort of women born in the 1920s and 1930s. These are the women whose mothers greeted their decision to seek paid employment with confusion and dismay, and whose daughters take it for granted that they will work outside the home most of their adult lives. Theirs are the marriages rocked by the contradiction between strict, conventional views of the division of labor between husband and wife within the home, on the one hand, and the family's need for the income of a second wage earner and the growth in employment opportunities for women on the other. These are the working wives who sacrificed sleep and leisure to fulfill their traditional role at home, averaging 71 hours of work each week at home and on the job, compared with 55 hours for their husbands. What explains their entrance in such large numbers into the work force after World War II?

Standard economic analysis of this question is both ahistorical and asocial. It casts the question of female labor force participation in terms of each individual woman's decision to allocate her time between work at home, paid employment, and leisure. Two opposing tendencies are identified. Rising real wages for women cause them to substitute paid employment for unpaid work at home or leisure-time activities. At the same time, a rise in family income, as husband's real wages increase, induces an "income effect" in which women choose leisure or home work over paid employment. Economists then interpret the rapid increase in labor force participation rates of married women in the postwar period as the triumph of the "substitution effect" over the "income effect." Had women not entered the labor force in such numbers, traditional economic theory would have celebrated the victory of the "income effect" over the "substitution effect" with equal fervor. The choice theoretic framework is thus consistent with either increases or no increase in female labor force participation rates. It cannot, therefore, serve as an explanation of the changed relationship between women and work.

An answer to the question of why so many women now work outside the home requires a re-examination of the assumptions underlying the traditional view of sex roles within the family. As I argue in the first chapter, the increased requirements of industry for women workers in the 1950s and 1960s and the slowdown in the growth of real income in the 1970s challenged these assumptions and set in motion a complicated social and economic dynamic out of which emerged the influx of wives and mothers into the labor force. The increase in the participation of women in paid employment is analyzed in that chapter in the context of the major economic events of the last 35 years, with special attention to the interaction between the family as a social institution and the changing economic environment. It is undeniable that individual women do make choices and decisions regarding labor supply. But these decisions are made in an historical and institutional milieu and are dictated as often as not by necessity. The actions of groups of women, therefore, cannot be fully understood or interpreted without reference to the historically specific context in which their decisions are taken.

One point that becomes evident from the historical discussion is that the "working wife phenomenon" is not really a single phenomenon at all; rather, it is two distinct phenomena. For, over the life cycle, married women who work can be observed to follow one or the other of two very different patterns of paid employment. In the first pattern, mothers stay home for an extended period following the birth of their first child, re-entering the labor force when their children are in school. In the second pattern, mothers work outside the home even when their children are young. Casual observation suggests that the labor market experiences of these two groups of women may be quite different; but little is actually known about the implications for married women of pursuing one or the other of these work and family patterns. What, for example, are the long-run economic costs of giving up a job and staying home while the children are young? Are women in the two groups equally satisfied with their jobs, and are the factors that contribute to job satisfaction the same in both cases? What about the things that women do to improve their skills and prepare for a return to the work force—do any of them help? And how do women who re-enter the labor force seeking part-time work in order to cope, perhaps, with competing demands on their time, or to bridge their return to the world of market work, make out in that world?

The answers to these questions ought to be of interest to those charged with formulating policies to meet the needs of women in the last two decades of this century. They are undoubtedly of pressing concern to young women, born in the 1950s and 1960s, who are currently contemplating work and family decisions. It may be instructive to them to see how the generation that preceded them, their mothers' generation, fared in the labor market; and what profound effect the pattern of employment over the life cycle had.

The issues raised here are of more than passing interest to me for it is the experiences of my cohort, the generation of women who were born before World War II and who first swelled the ranks of the labor force in the decades after it, that are to be examined. We have reached an age now when we can look back on our lives and take stock. It is appropriate that we begin to systematize what we have culled from our experiences and make it available to women who are just beginning their work lives.

This book is part of that process. It is not, however, a personal statement. Rather, it attempts to capture more generally the experiences of my generation through an analysis of data from a national sample of women. It may, nevertheless, be of some interest to readers to know what my own pattern of employment has been.

I belong to the group of women who worked even while their children were young, having left the labor force only briefly following the births of each of my three children. This was a course of action, I might add, that appalled my parents. Those two caring and decent people, who had in their own lives practiced a very traditional division of labor, had always encouraged me to pursue my intellectual interests, never suggesting that I channel my energies into fields more suitable for a woman. It wasn't until years later that I learned that this was because it never occurred to either of them that a daughter of theirs might work. My husband brought to our marriage a commitment, learned at his mother's knee, to the ideal that responsibility for the day-to-day care of children and for their financial support belonged to both parents. In the twenty-one years since we married, we have endeavored to build a family unit that would support the aspirations of each of its members. In the absence of a system of social supports for families in which both parents work, this has often required heroic sacrifices on the part of one parent or the other and the postponement, sometimes indefinitely, of cherished plans. As the children have grown older, it has also required that they assume a major portion of the burden of housekeeping tasks.

In the absence of adequate child care facilities and a social structure molded around the premise of working parents, conflicts between the demands of work and of family life are inevitable, and disappointments are bound to occur. But if individual families cannot by themselves resolve the problems inherent under these circumstances in combining work and children, they can at least function so that the burdens do not fall unfairly on any one family member. This much we have accomplished.

The existence of this book owes much to the willingness of the members of my family to delay their own plans in order to facilitate the accomplishment of mine. I gratefully acknowledge their help, support, and patience.

EILEEN APPELBAUM
April 1, 1981

CONTENTS

Chapter 1

CHANGING WORK
AND FAMILY ROLES
OF MARRIED WOMEN

The broad social and economic changes that swept across the United States in the 1960s and 1970s found expression in the shifting personal and economic fortunes of individual Americans. Economic events—including the long-overdue end of the nation's most protracted war, the sharp jump in energy prices in 1973 and again in 1979, the slowdown in the rate of productivity growth, the onset of the steepest inflation since World War II, a mild recession in 1969–1970, and the deepest recession since the Great Depression in 1973–1975—altered the lives and threatened the economic well-being of a great many individuals. In the face of these events the American family, as an institution, did not remain invulnerable to change. Under the unremitting pressure on the American standard of living in the last decade the influx of wives into the labor force, which began in earnest after World War II, continued apace. The dramatic increase between 1965 and 1975 in the proportion of married women with children under the age of six in the labor force was of even greater significance. By 1979, 4.8 million married women with young children, comprising 43.2 percent of all women with children under six, were working or looking for a job. Both the number and the proportion of wives with young children who worked for wages quadrupled between 1948, when these data first became available, and 1979. Moreover, among mothers with dependent children age six and older, 59.1 percent were in the labor

Table 1-1 Wives in the Labor Force, by Presence and Age of Children

	1948	1950	1955	1960	1965	1970	1975	1976	1977	1978	1979
Number of wives (thousands):	7,553	8,550	10,423	12,253	14,708	18,377	21,143	21,554	22,377	22,789	23,832
With no children under 18	4,400	4,946	5,227	5,692	6,755	8,174	9,718	9,860	10,268	10,320	10,974
With children 6–17 only	1,927	2,205	3,183	4,087	4,836	6,289	6,988	7,270	7,674	7,829	8,064
With children under 6	1,226	1,399	2,012	2,474	3,117	3,914	4,438	4,424	4,435	4,640	4,795
Labor force participation rate (percent) of wives:	22.0	23.8	27.7	30.5	34.7	40.8	44.4	45.0	46.6	47.6	49.4
With no children under 18	28.4	30.3	32.7	34.9	38.3	42.2	43.9	43.8	44.9	44.7	46.7
With children 6–17 only	26.0	28.3	34.7	39.0	42.7	49.2	52.3	53.7	55.6	57.2	59.1
With children under 6	10.8	11.9	16.2	18.6	23.3	30.3	36.6	37.4	39.3	41.6	43.2

SOURCE: U.S. Department of Labor, Bureau of Labor Statistics, *Handbook of Labor Statistics*, December 1980, Table 57.

Note: These figures are as of March, except for 1948 and 1955, which are as of April. Data prior to 1960 excludes Alaska and Hawaii.

force in 1979 (Table 1-1). As a result, the definition of woman primarily as mother—with major responsibility for child rearing, with only a secondary interest in paid employment, and economically dependent on her husband, especially when her children are young—cannot be sustained in an increasing number of cases. Instead, women are spending more years in the labor force and, increasingly, are engaged in paid employment continuously over their work lives regardless of whether they marry or have children. Whether or not the conflict between paid employment, motherhood, and unpaid domestic service to the family is resolved in particular cases, it seems clear that the new reality of women's employment conflicts both with conventional perceptions of women's role in the family and with the structure of employment opportunities for women. Both family and labor market institutions are experiencing simultaneous pressures to accommodate change and to resist it.

Traditional conceptualizations of the division of labor between the sexes, in which men assume the role of economic provider while women perform unpaid housework and child care within the family, are currently being re-examined in light of the employment of wives and mothers. That traditional view of sex roles rested on two presuppositions, both of which have been challenged by events of the last 35 years. The first assumption was that the requirements of business and industry for labor could largely be met out of the available pool of male workers. The second was that men were able to command a market wage sufficient, in combination with the unpaid labor provided by their wives in processing and preparing food and clothing, in raising children, and in household care and maintenance, to meet their own needs and those of their families. The bringing forth of each new generation of men with the requisite education and labor market skills and of women appropriate to marry them and bear their children could, it was assumed, safely be left to the population's instincts for propagation and self-preservation.

As we shall demonstrate in this chapter, these assumptions have been seriously undermined by developments since the late 1940s, with important consequences both for women's employment patterns and for women's roles within the family.

The Sexual Division of Labor in the Early Decades
of the Twentieth Century

While the traditional description of the American family has never
been entirely accurate—it blatantly disregarded the historical experience of black families in America, and conveniently overlooked the
plight of families deserted by husbands who could not or would not
support them—this view of married women as engaged in work
within the home served rather well for the nineteenth century and
for the first four decades of the twentieth. In 1890 only 4.6 percent
of all married women were engaged in paid employment. This figure
increased gradually to 13.8 percent by 1940 (Table 1-2). Census data
prior to 1940 do not indicate how many of these women had dependent children at home, but the proportion of married women
with children who worked for pay must have been small indeed. In

Table 1-2   Women in the Civilian Labor Force: 1890–1979[a]

Decennial Census	Labor Force Participation Rate			Proportion of Labor Force Who Are Women	
	All Women	Married Women[b]	Women Aged 25–44 Years	All Women	Married Women[b]
1979[c]	50.7	49.4	63.4	42.2	23.1
1970 (April)	41.6	39.6	47.5	37.2	21.4
1960 (April)[d]	34.5	30.6	39.1	32.1	17.9
1950 (April)	29.0	21.6	33.3	27.8	13.0
1940 (April)	25.8	13.8	30.5	24.6	7.4
1930 (April)	24.8	11.7	24.6	21.9	6.5
1920 (January)	23.7	9.0	21.7	20.4	4.8
1910 (April)[e]	25.4	10.7	n.a.	n.a.	n.a.
1900 (June)	20.6	5.6	17.5	18.1	2.8
1890 (June)	18.9	4.6	15.1	17.0	2.4

SOURCE: U.S. Dept. of Commerce, Bureau of the Census, *Historical Statistics of the United
States, Colonial Times to 1970* (Series D49-62 for col. 1 and 2; Series D29-41 for col. 3; Series
D49-62 for col. 4; Series D29-41 for col. 5) for the years from 1890 to 1970. Data for 1979 are
from U.S. Dept. of Commerce, Bureau of the Census, *Statistical Abstract of the United States
1980* (Table 668 for columns 1 and 2; Table 653 for column 3; Table 652 for column 4; Tables
652 and 671 for column 5).
[a] Persons 15 years old and over, 1890–1930; 14 years old and over, 1940–1950; 16 years old
and over thereafter.
[b] All married, 1890–1930; married women, husband present, thereafter.
[c] Data for 1979 are from the Bureau of Labor Statistics and are not strictly comparable with
data from the Decennial Census.
[d] First year for which figures include Alaska and Hawaii.
[e] Data are not comparable with earlier or later censuses due to differences in enumeration.
Many women, particularly agricultural laborers, who would not have been enumerated in
other censuses were enumerated as gainful workers.

terms of their representation in the labor force, married women accounted for a mere 3 percent of the total at the turn of the century, and as recently as 1940 they comprised only about 7.5 percent of it. Paid employment of women was not unknown during this period—nearly one fifth of women in 1890 and one fourth of them in 1940 were gainfully employed—but it was confined largely to single women. On becoming a wife, a woman was expected to put aside other preoccupations and assume lifelong responsibilities for home and family; and most, in fact, did.

Reasons for Leaving Paid Employment

Among the factors that led women to leave paid employment upon marriage, two in particular stand out. Women's wages were considered to be supplementary to the family's income and were low both in comparison with men's wages and with the cost of the woman's own subsistence. For married women whose husbands were employed, therefore, the alternatives were poorly paying jobs in the labor market or productive activity in the household in the service of husbands who could command a higher market wage. In the decades before industry supplied processed foods and mass-produced clothing relatively cheaply and on a large scale, women could contribute more to their family's consumption by working in the home rather than in the marketplace. At the same time, employers preferred to hire young single girls, many of whom migrated to the cities from rural areas in response to the availability of jobs. Clerical and sales positions were often restricted to single women, domestic servants were sometimes required to live in, and nurses and teachers were discouraged from marrying. Thus marriage meant a decline in employment opportunities.

For women, then, there was no real choice. Paid employment was simply the stage in the life cycle between leaving school and marriage. The differential between the wages of men and women and the lack of jobs for married women reinforced a sexual division of labor in which women performed unpaid labor in the home while men worked outside the home for wages, and in which married women were economically dependent on their husbands. Meanwhile, dependence of women on the family unit for financial support was used to rationalize the payment of low wages to them and to justify their utilization by employers as cheap labor. The low wages paid to women and the reluctance of firms to employ married women meant that wives worked only in the event that their husbands were ill, unemployed, or poorly paid. Pressure on married women to continue working was an indication of household need. In these desperate circumstances, married women took what jobs they could find, working for low wages and in conditions that threatened their stamina and their health. Employment was low-paying, irregular, and intermittent—gladly given up when the emergency passed.

With paid employment of women in the late nineteenth and early twentieth centuries limited largely to single women and, in particular, *young* single women who were confidently expected to marry and withdraw from the labor force, it is not surprising that women were confined to jobs that were viewed as consistent with their place in the family and with the existing sexual division of labor in the home. Thus jobs that were an extension of women's traditional caring and nurturing roles—household service, making apparel, canning fruits, nursing, teaching young children—were labeled "women's work." The sex labeling of occupations that effectively restricted women to jobs that were consonant with their role in society went on at a more subtle level as well.[1] The dominant role of men within the family and the submissive role of women would have been threatened if women held positions of authority when they worked. Thus supervisory functions, even where the work force was predominantly female, were the domain of male workers. Additionally, women were expected to achieve satisfaction indirectly through the successes of their husbands and sons, not through their own accomplishments. Vicarious achievement for women was perpetuated in occupations characterized as "female": the secretary who was expected to help her boss succeed, the nurse who was expected to assist the doctor in patient care, and even the teacher whose goal was to help her students succeed. Thus occupational segregation, which limited women to "women's work" (Table 1-3), supported traditional sex roles and the division of labor within the home.

The Sexual Division of Labor 1948–1965

With some amendment the traditional view of women's role as located in the home, providing domestic service and raising children, survived both the mobilization of workers (including married women) for wartime production in the early 1940s and the rapid rise

Table 1-3 Employment of Women in Selected Occupations, 1900–1979

Occupation	Number of Women (in thousands)							Women as Percent of All Workers in Occupation						
	1900	1930	1940	1950	1960	1970	1979	1900	1930	1940	1950	1960	1970	1979
Professional-technical	434	1,482	1,608	1,946	2,746	4,576	6,519	35.2	44.8	41.5	40.1	38.0	40.0	43.3
Accountants				56	77	180	344				14.9	16.4	25.3	32.9
Engineers				6	8	20	40				1.2	0.9	1.6	2.9
Lawyers-judges				7	7	13	62				4.1	3.3	4.7	12.4
Physicians-osteopaths				12	16	25	46				6.5	6.8	8.9	10.7
Registered nurses				394	567	814	1,184				97.8	97.6	97.4	96.8
Teachers, except college and university				837	1,196	1,937	2,207				74.5	71.6	70.4	70.8
Teachers, college and university				28	36	139	172				22.8	21.3	28.3	31.6
Technicians, excluding medical-dental				21	44	49	199				20.6	12.8	14.5	16.1
Writers-artists-entertainers				50	82	229	470				40.3	34.2	30.1	37.8
Managerial-administrative, except farm	74	292	414	672	780	1,061	2,586	4.4	8.1	11.0	13.8	14.4	16.6	24.6
Bank officials-financial managers				13	28	55	196				11.7	12.2	17.6	31.6
Buyers-purchasing agents				6	61	75	136				9.4	17.7	20.8	30.2
Food service workers				93	141	109	224				27.1	24.0	33.7	35.4
Sales managers-department heads; retail trade				35	68	51	135				24.6	28.2	24.1	39.8
Sales	228	736	925	1,314	1,646	2,143	2,779	17.4	24.1	26.8	34.5	36.6	39.4	45.1
Sales representatives (including wholesale)				37	70	76	162				5.2	7.3	7.2	12.4
Sales clerks, retail				1,175	1,384	1,465	1,671				48.9	53.7	64.8	70.7
Clerical	212	2,246	2,700	4,273	6,263	10,150	14,152	24.2	51.8	54.2	62.3	67.5	73.6	80.3
Bank tellers				28	88	216	458				45.2	69.3	86.1	92.9
Bookkeepers				556	764	1,274	1,740				77.7	83.4	82.1	91.1
Cashiers				187	367	692	1,298				81.7	78.4	84.0	87.9
Office machine operators				116	225	414	677				81.1	73.8	73.5	74.9
Secretaries-typists				1,494	1,917	3,686	4,681				94.6	96.7	96.6	98.6
Shipping-receiving clerks				19	24	59	103				14.3	8.6	14.3	21.3

Table 1-3 (continued)

Occupation	Number of Women (in thousands)							Women as Percent of All Workers in Occupation						
	1900	1930	1940	1950	1960	1970	1979	1900	1930	1940	1950	1960	1970	1979
Craft	76	106	135	236	252	518	737	2.5	1.7	2.2	3.1	2.9	4.9	5.7
Carpenters				4	3	11	16				0.4	0.4	1.3	1.3
Mechanics, including auto-motive				21	25	49	49				1.2	1.1	2.0	1.4
Printing				35	35	58	101				11.8	11.0	14.8	22.2
Bakers				14	17	32	61				12.2	15.9	29.4	43.6
Decorators and window dressers				14	24	42	94				32.6	46.2	58.3	72.9
Tailors				16	8	22	12				19.8	20.2	31.4	34.3
Upholsterers				5	6	10	12				8.3	10.0	16.4	21.4
Operatives, except transport				2,995	3,252	4,036	4,353				33.5	34.3	38.4	39.9
Assemblers				N.A.	267	459	688				N.A.	43.7	48.7	53.4
Bottling and canning operatives				N.A.	N.A.	16	17				N.A.	N.A.	34.0	37.8
Clothing ironers and pressers				N.A.	N.A.	137	89				N.A.	N.A.	74.9	76.8
Dressmakers				135	116	92	104				97.1	96.7	94.8	95.4
Laundry and dry cleaning operatives				288	273	105	122				67.7	71.3	62.9	65.9
Sewers and stitchers				N.A.	532	816	772				N.A.	94.0	93.8	95.3
Transport equipment operatives				22	41	134	294				1.0	1.7	4.5	8.1
Bus drivers				4	18	68	163				2.6	9.8	28.5	45.5
Operatives (inclusive)	1,264	1,870	2,452					34.0	24.3	25.8				
Service	1,886	2,954	3,699	3,228	4,418	5,944	8,011	71.8	61.9	60.9	54.3	62.8	60.5	62.4
Private household	1,526	1,909	2,277	1,321	1,596	1,132	1,062	96.6	95.5	94.4	94.9	96.6	96.9	97.6
Food service				839	1,379	1,913	2,943				61.6	70.0	68.8	68.4
Health service				249	488	1,047	1,643				74.6	81.5	88.0	90.4
Personal service				221	326	778	1,369				49.7	57.9	66.5	77.3
Protective service				11	28	59	124				2.0	4.1	6.2	8.8

SOURCES: U.S. Department of Commerce, Bureau of the Census, *Historical Statistics of the United States: Colonial Times to 1970*, Series D182-232, for 1900–1940. U.S. Department of Labor, Bureau of Labor Statistics, *Perspectives on Working Women: A Databook*, October 1980, Bulletin 2080, Table 11, for 1950–1979.

in the demand for labor in the two decades of exceptional economic growth following World War II. Marriage remained the basic component of the female role, household responsibilities were expected to come first, and a mother's place while her children were young was assumed to be in the home. Nevertheless, it became increasingly acceptable for married women to undertake paid employment if their primary obligations could still be met. The exigencies of wartime production forced a temporary relaxation of social pressures against the employment of married women, and labor force participation rates of wives increased substantially between 1940 and 1944 reaching 22 percent in 1944.[2] The conclusion of the war amidst gloomy predictions of renewed recession and depression brought numerous calls for women to leave industrial jobs and return to their traditional roles in order to facilitate the demobilization of veterans. The participation rate for wives declined between 1944 and 1947, though it remained well above its 1940 level. It was the unexpected and unprecedented expansion of the economy and the resulting labor shortage in the postwar period that provided not only employment opportunities for married women, but a sympathetic economic environment for the shift in ideology that enabled them to enter the labor force.

Amendment, though not any fundamental revision, of the accepted role for married women was necessitated by the inability of business and industry to meet rapidly growing labor requirements out of the slowly growing pool of single women.[3] The supply of male workers grew slowly in the period from 1945 to 1965 as the result of several factors. The low birth rate from 1930 to 1945 reduced the number of young men available to work in the next two decades, as did the increased proportion of young men enrolled in postsecondary education, while casualties during World War II reduced the number of men in their twenties and early thirties. The result was that employers had difficulty filling even traditionally male jobs from the available supply of men. The low birth rate affected the supply of young single women as well, and the proportion of eighteen- and nineteen-year-old women enrolled in college increased. In addition, age at first marriage declined between 1940 and 1950, and, between 1945 and 1955, birth rates jumped. Employment of single women declined from 6.7 million in 1940 to 5.1 million in 1955, and increased to only 5.9 million by 1965. The major increase during these decades in service, sales, and clerical occupations could not be filled, except by married women.

Thus, expansion of the economy in the decades immediately following World War II provided the initial impetus and opportunity
for married women to engage in paid employment. Rapid growth in
clerical, sales, and service employment followed as national and local
governments provided additional services to the public, administrative bureaucracies accompanied the growth in scale of private enterprises, and an enlarged system of distribution was necessitated by
expanded production of manufactured goods and of food products.
Growth in this sector of the economy, which began in the early
decades of the twentieth century, accelerated after 1948. Clerical
and sales positions were transformed from positions appropriate for
educated and aspiring young men into low-skill, white-collar jobs
and were feminized early in the twentieth century as employers
recruited unskilled, single women, to whom very low wages could
be paid, to fill them. The rapid growth in the number of clerical,
sales, and service jobs in the postwar period occurred just as the pool
of single women, who were preferred for these jobs, was declining.
Slow growth in the pool of male workers, which just kept pace with
the growth of traditionally male jobs, and the low wages associated
with the new clerical, sales, and service positions precluded the
possibility that young men would be attracted to them. Employers
turned to married women to make up the labor deficit, hiring them
for jobs in occupations that by 1940 were already labeled "female."
While the overall labor force participation rate for women increased
only 6 percentage points, from 32 percent in 1948 to 38 percent in
1965,[4] the labor force participation rate for married women increased from 22 percent to 35 percent. Among married women
whose youngest child was already in school the increase in the labor
force participation rate was even greater, rising from 26 percent in
1948 to 43 percent in 1965 (see Table 1-1). By 1970 a married woman
with children could expect to spend 25 years in the labor force.[5]

Labor Requirements versus Traditional Roles

A complicated dynamic was set in motion during these two decades
by the tension between the high demand for female labor generated
by a rapidly expanding economy and the expectation that married
women would continue to fulfill their traditional role as housewives.
The dominant view that emerged, held not only by husbands but by
employers and often by the women themselves, was that female
employment was acceptable provided that it was subordinated to the

claims of domesticity. As recently as 1964, only 54 percent of women in a national survey agreed that a mother who worked could still establish a close relationship with her children, and even this represented a major change in attitude when compared with views held 30 years earlier.[6] The entrance of married women into the labor force in the postwar decades was conditioned by the widely held belief that paid employment for such women was incidental to their primary roles as wives and mothers, and was subordinate in importance to their responsibilities at home.[7] Popular ideology endorsed the view that men were to be the chief providers and that women, even when they worked, were to be dependent on the earnings of husbands or fathers for part of their support. Disparities in wage rates between men and women guaranteed that this would, by and large, be the case.

The acceptance of this formulation of the appropriate roles for men and women had implications on many levels. In families where both husband and wife worked, the wife commonly continued to provide nearly all domestic services—shopping, cooking, cleaning, laundry, and child care. Married women who worked outside the home received little additional help with household work from their husbands.

A study of household production of family goods and services in the mid-1960s found that wives with children worked in the home a minimum of 36 hours each week, on average, whether or not they were employed.[8] While working wives spent 19 fewer hours on housework and child care than did full-time homemakers, the total time spent by employed wives working in the home and on the job averaged 71 hours each week. In comparison, husbands of working wives spent, on average, only 55 hours in work at home and on the job. Husbands spent an average of 11 hours a week helping in the home—mainly with yard and car care, home maintenance, marketing, and nonphysical care of children—whether their wives were employed full-time, worked part time, or were full-time homemakers. Meal preparation and cleanup, physical care of children and family members, clothing care, and regular housework remained the responsibility of wives. In addition, they fulfilled their dual obligations by using part of their earnings to substitute market goods for home production (packaged bread for home baked, store-bought clothes for homemade, restaurant meals for home cooked) and by reducing the amount of time spent sleeping and in "passive leisure," reading or watching TV.[9]

The husband, whose job was held to matter, could not be expected to dissipate energy and initiative providing domestic services to his family. On the contrary, his wife was still expected to behave so as to expedite and advance his possibilities for success or advancement at work. This included leaving her job to follow him if his employment required moves across the country, leaving her job when children were born and remaining at home while they were young, and, in general, leaving her job whenever serious work-family conflicts arose. The low wages commanded by most women and their continued economic dependence upon their husbands' earnings even when they worked precluded any other arrangement. The result is not difficult to anticipate: Married women tended to work intermittently, moving into and out of the labor force in response to changes in their situation at home. Whatever their personal aspirations, many of them found it difficult to exhibit a commitment to a career, a desire for seniority, or an interest in long-term opportunities for advancement. Essentially, it was employment outside the home by married women who had no children, or whose children were all in school, that came to be viewed as consistent with the presumably more compelling obligations of marriage. Thus the net increase in the late 1940s and through the decade of the 1950s in the proportion of wives in the labor force was marked by a notable increase in the participation rates of women between 45 and 59 years of age, whose child-rearing responsibilities occupied substantially less of their time. Even in this period, however, an increase in the number of married women with preschool age children who worked can be observed. In addition, women returning to work often sought part-time employment as a means of reconciling their work schedules with the conflicting demands of home and family.

Differences in Wages Paid to Men and Women

A second consequence of sustaining the ideology that men should be the chief providers and that women should be economically dependent on them was that this view then functioned (as it had in the earlier period) as a justification for the payment of low wages to women. Wages paid to women were seen as supplementing those paid to men. The payment of wages to women insufficient to provide a decent standard of living was made possible by the existence of the family and the presumed dependence of women upon their husbands' wages for a major part of their support. Despite an increase in the real wages of women, occasioned perhaps by the increase in demand for female labor, the median earnings of women employed full-time, year-round, averaged (and still average) about 60 percent of those of men. A startling observation is that contemporary records show that women's wages were set at 60 percent of men's as early as the Industrial Revolution in nineteenth-century England.[10] The income needs of single women were assumed to be less than the needs of men with families to support, while married women, it was assumed, were provided for by their husbands. The wages of women thus have largely been culturally determined. Moreover, this tendency to underpay women on the assumption that a major share of their support was contributed by men has been responsible, in this century and the last, for much of the poverty of single women, widows, and their families who, in fact, must manage without a male wage.

Employment of Women and Labor Market Segmentation

Possibly the most far-reaching consequence of sustaining traditional societal views of male and female sex roles while recruiting an increasing number of married women into the labor force was the effect on the structure of jobs in the American economy. Women were integrated into the work force through an expansion in the number of low-paying, dead-end jobs; and labor market segmentation increased.

The segmentation of the labor market into submarkets characterized by differences in wages, working conditions, and opportunities for advancement originated several decades prior to the economic expansion of the postwar period and the increase in the numbers of married women in the work force. To a large extent, labor market segmentation arose as part of the historical process that led to the development of technologically advanced, oligopolistic firms at the core of the economy and smaller firms lacking technological sophistication on the periphery.[11] As a result of technological advances, the production processes in some firms became increasingly complex, hierarchical, and interdependent. The specific skills needed by many workers in these firms could only be learned through continuous tenure on a particular job or with a particular firm. Thus firms utilizing modern technologies have had an incentive to encourage stable work histories for workers in jobs in which productivity is related to tenure. This entailed adjustments in working conditions, monetary rewards, and a system of promotion to higher status jobs. Career ladders are especially important in this context since they serve both to stratify workers and to keep them attached to the same firm for longer periods of time. Differentiated job categories, therefore, were created by modern firms whether required by technology or not.

Providing good working conditions, higher wages, on-the-job training, and opportunities for advancement is costly to firms. The other side of the coin, therefore, is that smaller firms on the periphery of the economy have been unable to provide such amenities for their workers. More important, even technologically advanced firms have had an incentive to restrict those extra expenses to as narrow a range of jobs as possible. Thus even the most modern firms have created highly stratified internal job clusters with different entry requirements. Some strategic work sectors within these firms have been organized to encourage job stability and others to permit highly unstable work behavior. The result has been a labor market segmented into a primary sector, in which stable work habits are rewarded, and a secondary sector, in which turnover is high and stability is neither required nor encouraged.

Segmentation predates the movement of married women into the labor force, but the structure of jobs was very much affected by the fact that married women were the main pool of labor available to be tapped in the years from 1945 to 1965. The prevailing ideology, which held that women should leave paid employment to have children and should drop out of the labor force as required by the demands of family and home responsibility, was used by employers to justify denying women training opportunities and barring them from access to jobs that provide on-the-job training. Additionally, firms interpreted traditional sex role attitudes to mean that supervisory responsibilities should be given to men, not women. Moreover, as the economy grew and the employment of married women increased, employers had both an opportunity and an incentive to structure as many of the new jobs as possible so that they could be performed by a low-paid, intermittent work force. A major aspect of this was the fragmentation and deskilling of tasks. In jobs for which women were to be recruited, employers had a socially acceptable justification for breaking up the production process—in offices and in retail stores, as well as in factories—into separate tasks, and for substituting routine, repetitive operations for craft skills or mental labor. Jobs were simultaneously deskilled and feminized. Techniques were developed and introduced that were designed to be easily mastered by quickly trained female labor. Women were rarely hired directly into jobs that had previously been identified as "male" jobs. Instead, new jobs were created and designated as "female" work that were subordinate not only in terms of the lesser skills required for them, but also because of the subordinate social status ascribed to women. Thus the fact that married women were the most readily available source of workers to meet the expanding labor requirements of the economy in this period, together with the dominant ideological view that paid employment was a secondary role for women, led to the extension of segmented labor markets, and to the consignment of women to the secondary sector.

In the case of women, labor market segmentation, which was essentially concerned with the structuring of a significant proportion of jobs so that they required a minimum of skills and so that production was insulated from the effects of high turnover, was compounded by occupational segregation. Historically, women had been limited to jobs that did not threaten traditional conceptions of the sexual division of labor in the home. The stereotyping of both blue- and white-collar jobs open to women, according to particular attributes commonly believed to be "feminine," continued in the 1950s and 1960s even as the employment of women grew. Thus women were limited by labor market segmentation to jobs in the secondary sector that required little beyond basic literacy, and that provided no development of skills on the job, no opportunities for advancement, and no rewards for long or loyal service.

Women were further limited by occupational segregation to a narrow range of jobs within the secondary sector. The low-skill requirements of the work for which women were recruited, the presumed intermittent nature of the female labor force, and the sex labeling of jobs, combined with the dominant view that paid employment by women was secondary to work within the family and that women's wages were of secondary importance to family income, provided employers with both the rationale and the means for paying low wages to women. Wages pegged at 60 percent of the average wage of male workers, after all, could not have been offered to men. Yet it was precisely the payment of low wages that guaranteed women a second-class position in the labor market and a dependent status in marriage. Low wages were both cause and effect of the low status of women and of women's work. Moreover, the assignment of women to low-paying jobs, in which neither wage increases nor promotions reward long service, has been a cause of the high turnover rates observed among these workers. Women, like men in such jobs, correctly recognize that there is little to be gained from continuing in the same job. Though turnover rates have been about the same for women as for men in jobs of similar status, the heavy concentration of women in dead-end jobs has tended to reinforce the impression that women are casual workers, lack commitment to their jobs, and have unstable work histories. High turnover, which resulted in part from the character of jobs in the secondary labor market to which women were assigned, was then used by employers as sufficient reason to deny women access to more responsible positions.

Though married women were recruited into the labor force by the millions during this period—the number of working wives increased from 7.6 million in 1948 to 14.7 million in 1965[12]—the structure of job opportunities for women had the effect of sustaining the traditional division of labor by sex within the home. Extensive segmentation of the labor market, occupational segregation by sex, and the deskilling of jobs labeled "female" effectively denied women opportunities for training, advancement, or a career. The dead-end, unrewarding nature of jobs designed for a work force that was presumed to be intermittent encouraged high turnover rates among women. The low wages and low status associated with jobs held by women reinforced the view that paid employment for women was secondary to providing domestic service to husbands and other family members. Moreover, the low wages commanded by women in the labor market meant that, while family income increased by 25 to 30 percent as a result of the wife's contribution,[13] a wife remained dependent upon her husband's earnings for most of her own support and the support of her children. The high incidence of poverty in families that lacked the financial support of a male wage earner provided a lesson whose meaning was not lost upon married women. Divorce rates were higher in 1965 than they were in the early decades of the twentieth century, but, contrary to popular impression, divorce rates declined steadily between 1948 and 1965. The wartime peak was slightly higher than 4 divorces per thousand population, while by 1965 the divorce rate had declined to 2.5 divorces per thousand population.[14] Evidence regarding the conten-

tion that marriages in which the wife worked outside
more likely to end in divorce than those in which
full-time homemaker is, at best, inconclusive; and s
families in the 1950s and 1960s found that marital stability,
affected by the wife's employment.[15]

Effect of Women's Employment on Standard of Living

Thus, despite the dramatic increase in paid employment of married
women in the two decades following World War II, the subordinate
position of women within the family and their second-class status
within the labor market remained largely unchanged. That statement should not be interpreted to mean, however, that no
significant changes in the social fabric were wrought by the increase
in the number of working wives. While a wife's earnings were usually below even her own subsistence, they were nevertheless
sufficiently high to affect her family's standard of living. The advent
of the multiple-earner family in which both husband and wife
worked had a major impact on family income and consumption expenditures. The average upper-middle-income household with a
working wife would have dropped to middle-income status without
the wife's paycheck, while the average middle-income family with a
working wife would have fallen to lower-middle-income status if the
wife stopped working. Moreover, the wife's earnings were not
treated as "pin money," but were spent on those items that make up
the greater part of any family's expenditures—food, shelter, transportation, clothing, recreation, and Social Security and retirement.[16] The meaning and importance of this development did not
become fully apparent until inflation, recession, and slow productivity growth threatened the standard of living of American families
in the 1970s.

Legal and Social Changes Affecting Women after the Mid-1960s

The years from 1948 to 1965 were characterized not only by economic expansion and employment growth in the "feminized sectors"
of the economy but by a relative increase in affluence as well. After

correcting for inflation, the spendable average weekly earnings of a worker with three dependents increased from $72.18 in 1950 to $82.25 in 1960, an increase of 14.0 percent over the decade. This was followed by a further 11.5 percent increase between 1960 and 1965, as real spendable weekly earnings reached $91.67.[17] The median money income of families rose even more dramatically over this period as, in addition to the rise in real wages, the employment of wives increased. Between 1950 and 1960 the median money income of families, after eliminating the effects of inflation, rose 37.6 percent; and between 1960 and 1965 median money income increased another 15.8 percent in real terms.[18] In this favorable economic context and against the backdrop of more than ten years of rising labor force participation rates for women, the women's movement re-emerged in the 1960s to press for the social, political, and economic equality of women.

Largely dormant after the victory of the suffragists in winning passage of the Nineteenth Amendment, the women's movement fell into disarray during the 1930s. It was impossible even to contemplate mounting a struggle for the economic emancipation of women during that grim Depression period. The social pressures to confine women strictly to the functions of wife and mother, and to keep them out of the labor force where they would have competed with men for scarce jobs and further strained the capacity of the economic system to provide jobs for all who sought work, were formidable. The arbitrary firing of married women was practiced by government and industry, and many married women were forced out of employment regardless of whether their families depended on their wages.[19] Women whose husbands were out of work or could not earn even a minimally adequate wage continued, as in the past, to seek gainful employment and found it, when it could be found at all, in menial or low-paying jobs as domestic or other service workers, factory operatives, or clerical workers (compare the occupational distribution of women workers in 1930 and 1940 in Table 1-3). But no breakthroughs in employment opportunities for women were possible in this decade, and only a small increase in the proportion of married women engaged in paid employment occurred. In contrast, the more hospitable economic climate of the 1950s gave rise, in the 1960s, to the renewed struggle by women (among others) for full equality.

Legal Changes Affecting Women

The most tangible result of this struggle, facilitated by the prolonged boom and the employment gains of women, was the rapid change in the legal environment. The so-called protective labor laws passed in the early decades of the century, which limited the hours a woman could work and instituted prohibitions against women lifting heavy objects, working at night, or working while pregnant, had made it legal for firms to refuse to hire women for certain jobs and had created a climate that sanctioned discrimination against women workers generally. But in the mid-1960s federal laws intended to obtain equality of treatment and opportunity for women workers were enacted. The two basic laws passed at that time were the Equal Pay Act of 1963 and Title VII of the Civil Rights Act of 1964. The Equal Pay Act mandated that men and women must receive the same pay if their jobs required equal skill, effort, and responsibility. However, it did not require equal employment opportunity in terms of hiring or access to jobs. Title VII closed this loophole by outlawing discrimination in hiring or firing, fringe benefits, promotions, training, or any other conditions of employment. Despite the intention of these laws, occupational segregation on the basis of sex has allowed employers to circumvent both of these Acts. It has enabled them to pay women less than men for comparable work and to deny women access to jobs with well-defined career ladders and promotion opportunities. Nevertheless, the principle that sex discrimination should be outlawed was well established after the mid-1960s.

Women's advocacy groups began working for further measures to plug loopholes and strengthen enforcement. As a result, numerous changes in laws and legislative initiatives were undertaken in the 1970s to eradicate discrimination and improve economic opportunities for women. The most important of these include the Equal Employment Opportunity Act of 1972, amending Title VII of the Civil Rights Act of 1964; the 1972 Amendments to the Equal Pay Act of 1963, which extended occupational coverage; the Women's Educational Equity Act of 1974, amended in 1978, which extended coverage to women teachers; the Equal Credit Act of 1974, which allowed married women to establish their own credit records; Public Law 95-555, 1978, which banned discrimination based on pregnancy; the Tax Reform Act of 1976 and the Revenue Act of 1978, which established tax credits for child care; and Amendments to the Comprehensive Employment and Training Act of 1973, targeting jobs and training for disadvantaged women, single parents, and displaced homemakers, and funds for research on flexitime and part-time work. On the other side of the ledger it must be noted that when Congress enacted a day-care program designed to increase the availability of child-care facilities, President Nixon vetoed it as inconsistent with his view of the family and its responsibility for child rearing; that the Supreme Court in 1976 upheld the constitutionality of disability insurance systems that deny benefits to women incapacitated by pregnancy or childbirth; and that the Equal Rights Amendment to the U.S. Constitution, first proposed in 1923 and finally approved by the House of Representatives in 1971 and the Senate in 1972, is floundering in its progress through the states and remains three states shy of the number required for ratification.

It can be argued that these laws have been effective in reducing discrimination in the legal sense, and certainly this is true of the most blatant forms of unfair treatment. However, the persistence of the sex labeling of jobs, the crowding of women into a handful of occupations, and the wage gap between male and female earnings all point to the fact that women still have not achieved equality of opportunity and treatment in the labor market. Nevertheless, the effect of these laws has been to create an environment in which sex discrimination in employment is no longer sanctioned, in which firms are required to initiate affirmative action to remedy the effects of past discrimination, and in which at least some women find more attractive career options open to them.

Changes in Social Patterns

Dramatic changes in social mores also occurred during this period. The rate of first marriages declined 30 percent, from an average of 122 per thousand single women 14 to 44 years of age in 1951–1953 to 85 per thousand in 1975–1977. The most precipitous drop occurred during the late 1970s when the marriage rate fell to 85 from 103 per thousand in 1972–1974.[20] During the same period, cohabitation outside marriage became increasingly widespread. The median age at first marriage, which was unchanged between 1950 and 1960 at 20.3 for women and 22.8 for men, began edging up in the 1960s. By 1970 it stood at 20.8 years for women and 23.2 years for men, and in 1978 the ages were 21.8 and 24.2 years respectively.[21] At the same time, married couples in their twenties delayed or postponed the birth of the first child and had fewer children. In 1967 just 45 percent of wives

18 to 24 years of age expected to have no more than two children. In 1971 the proportion of wives in that age category who expected to have no more than two children had reached 64 percent; and by 1977 the proportion of wives aged 18 to 24 who expected to have no more than two children stood at 74 percent.[22] Contraceptives became more generally available, and their use became more widespread. Legal abortions increased fivefold during the 1970s.[23] Births per thousand women 15 to 44 years declined almost 25 percent from 87.9 in 1970 to 66.4 in 1978; and the number of children in a family, which had averaged 2.3 in 1970, averaged only 1.9 in 1978.[24] In addition to changes in the marriage rate and birth rate, the divorce rate increased dramatically after 1965. The number of divorces per thousand married women 14 to 44 years old was 14 in 1939–1941, 17 in 1942–1944, jumped to a wartime peak of 24 in 1945–1947, and then ranged between 15 and 17 between 1948 and 1965. By 1972–1974, however, the divorce rate had doubled to 32 per thousand, and in 1975–1977 it reached 37.[25]

By 1965, when changes in patterns of marriage and divorce, in the timing of children, and in family size were first observable, one third of all wives and two fifths of wives whose youngest child was in school were working (see Table 1-1). The employment of married women, which before World War II had typically been limited to women whose husbands were unable to provide for the family's basic needs, extended during the period from 1948 to 1965 to women of all income levels, including women who in earlier decades would not have gone out to work. To a significant minority of young women coming to maturity in the 1960s, work appeared as an option to be combined with marriage or pursued instead of it. The availability of contraceptives and legal abortions facilitated the postponement of marriage and allowed families to plan the timing of their children. Women were able to delay marriage or childbirth until their situations at work were clearly established, and some women did, in fact, do so. Though most women held poorly paid positions, some were able to achieve economic independence. A resurgent women's movement encouraged women to resist their subordinate status in the family and on the job. And the rapidly changing legal environment—many of those very changes having been won by women's advocacy groups—provided women with a basis for believing that they could successfully resist second-class status, that they could advance in their jobs, that they could enjoy more equal relationships with their husbands. It was this combination of events—economic, legal, and ideological—that gave rise after 1965 to the observed changes in patterns of marriage, childbearing, and divorce.

Effect of Labor Trends on Marriage and the Family

Alarm at these trends derives from concern over what they may indicate about the future of marriage and the family. While traditional views of sex roles within the family and the division of labor within the home are proving difficult to sustain as the proportion of working wives increases (a point elaborated further in the next section), there is no evidence to support the contention that the family itself will not survive the increase in women's labor force participation. Postponement of marriage is evident in the increasing proportion of those under 30 years of age who have never married. At the same time, the proportion who reached age 40 without marrying was at an all-time low in the late 1970s. While this situation may change—one study predicts that as many as 7 percent of women born in the 1950s will not marry by age 40—the fact remains that nearly all women, whether or not they plan to work, will marry.[26] And, while divorce rates are high, remarriage frequently follows divorce. The remarriage rate of 134 remarriages per thousand divorced and widowed women 14 to 54 years old in 1975–1977 equaled that of the 1950s and early 1960s, though it represents a decline from the 1966–1968 peak of 166.[27] Similarly, while the evidence supports the contention that families are having fewer children and having them later, it also indicates that most families are having children. Only a small increase in voluntary childlessness is predicted for women born in the 1950s and marrying in the 1970s.[28] Instead, women in their late twenties and thirties are having the children they delayed having earlier. A large number of women born during the high point of the post–World War II baby boom will be in their prime childbearing years in the next decade. Even with family size remaining small, birth rates are expected to rise through the 1980s. By 1990 the preschool-age population is expected to be 23.3 million, approximately 37 percent more than in 1978.[29]

Thus, despite changes in the family life cycle, most adults still marry and have children; and the evidence suggests that American families are here to stay.[30] The family remains largely intact as the living arrangment to which most Americans are committed. It is the family as an institution, which assigns men to a dominant role and women to a subordinate one and which assigns men to market work and women to unpaid service within the home, that is being questioned with increasing frequency as women participate in paid employment. In particular, the increasing economic dependence of the family on a second paycheck since the late 1960s, the increase in employment of wives with young children, and the more continuous attachment of married women to the labor force have challenged traditional arrangements within the family and in the labor market.

Economic Necessity and the Employment of Young Wives and Mothers: 1965–1980

Even in the first half of the twentieth century, when married women did not ordinarily work outside the home, women were expected to work in the event that illness or bad times reduced their husbands' wages. Women were encouraged to learn to type or, in the case of middle-class women, to obtain a teaching certificate so that they would be prepared should the worst occur. Whatever the prevailing ideology, women have always worked when economic necessity left them no choice. But the perception that the family's economic survival depended on two incomes and the expectation that a woman would work for the better part of her married life are specifically the product of the 1970s. Married women, finding that their families required their earnings and that jobs continued to be available for them in the feminized sectors of the economy, remained in the labor force for longer periods of time. Young mothers were much less likely than their counterparts in the preceding two decades to leave the labor force for an extended period when a child was born. The work-life expectancy of women, particularly married women with children, registered a substantial increase, and by 1977 the average woman could expect to spend nearly 28 years in paid employment.[31] In 1975, for the first time, the dip in labor force participation rates among women 25 to 29 years of age, which had persisted through the 1950s and 1960s despite increasing labor force participation rates for women in every age category, was no longer observable (see Table 1-4). Some women in this age category had, of course, postponed marriage and childbearing. But to a large extent this change in labor force participation rates by age reflected a change in employment patterns as the proportion of young married women with preschool age children who remained at their jobs or left only briefly

Table 1-4 Labor Force Participation Rates of Women Aged 20 to 34 by Year of Birth—Annual Averages for Selected Years

Year of Birth	1955		1960		1965		1970		1975		1979	
	Age	Rate	Age	Rate	Age	Rate	Age	Rate	Age	Rate	Age	Rate
1931–1935	20–24	46.0	25–29	35.7	30–34	38.2						
1936–1940			20–24	46.2	25–29	38.9	30–34	44.7				
1941–1945					20–24	50.0	25–29	45.2	30–34	51.7		
1946–1950							20–24	57.8	25–29	57.0	30–34	61.8
1951–1955									20–24	64.1	25–29	65.7

SOURCE: U.S. Department of Labor, Bureau of Labor Statistics, *Perspectives on Working Women: A Databook*, October 1980, Bulletin 2080.

when their children were born increased.[32] This change in employment patterns was mirrored, of course, in the increased labor force
participation rates of wives with children under the age of six. The
proportion of married women who had young children and worked
outside the home had climbed steadily during the 1950s, but had
reached only 18.6 percent of such mothers by 1960. By 1970 the
proportion stood at 30.3 percent, and by 1979 it had reached 43.2
percent (see Table 1-1).

The threat to the traditional conceptualization of the appropriate
role for women implicit in this changed pattern of paid employment
of married women is of greater significance than that resulting from
the deferment of marriage and changes in life-style or from increased
divorce rates. The sexual division of labor in which the wife assumes
responsiblity for child care and for providing domestic services to
her husband to facilitate his success in the labor market cannot be
sustained when the wife works continuously, and the family must
acknowledge its economic dependence on her income and her continued success on the job. Nor can the definition of woman primarily
as mother, devoted exclusively to child rearing while her children
are young and with only a secondary interest in paid employment
after they reach school age, survive for long when mothers of young
children work outside the home, with nearly two thirds of those
employed working at full-time jobs.[33] Nor is the family the only
institution in which the underlying assumption that women should
be subordinate to men is challenged by the new pattern of labor
force participation. As women work more continuously and look
forward to spending 27.6 years in paid employment (the comparable
figure for men is 38.3 years),[34] they are less willing to accept the
dead-end jobs assigned to them on the assumption that they will
soon withdraw from the labor force. Employers can no longer use
the rationale that women work sporadically when denying them
opportunities for training and advancement. Occupational segregation—with women confined mainly to low-skill, low-paying,
low-status jobs—becomes increasingly difficult to justify. Thus the
new pattern of female employment has tended to undermine the
traditional, subordinate role of women in the family and in the labor
market. Unlike the increased labor force participation of women
returning to work after the most time-intensive period of child rearing was past, the increase in paid employment of wives with young
children cannot be reconciled easily with pre-existing perceptions of
the appropriate role for women. Changes in the legal environment

and the multifaceted struggle by women for more egalitarian treatment and increased options, while undeniably important, are not by
themselves sufficient to explain changes in women's employment
patterns that run counter to the prevailing ideology. What, then,
accounts for this development?

Shrinking Real Wages and the Pattern of Women's Employment

As we argued earlier, one of the basic assumptions underlying the
traditional conceptualization of the division of labor between the
sexes was the supposition that men were able to command a market
wage sufficient, in combination with the unpaid labor performed by
their wives within the home, to meet the needs of their families. In
the 1970s, for the first time since the Depression, economic events
conspired to violate that assumption and to jeopardize the standard
of living of American families. Unlike the Depression era, however,
there was no scarcity of jobs for women this time. Though overall
economic activity was sluggish after 1973, the sex labeling of jobs
operated perversely to protect the employment position of women.

Though the economic boom continued through the 1960s, buoyed
up after 1965 by the Vietnam War, there was at least one early
indication that the post–World War II growth of affluence was
coming to an end. Spendable average weekly earnings of a worker
with three dependents peaked in 1965 at $91.67 in real terms, de-
clining steadily during the rest of that decade to $90.20 in 1970.[35]
Median money income of families continued to increase during this
period, however, at least in part because of the continued increase in
two-earner families. The labor force participation rate of wives
whose children were all in school approached 50 percent by 1970
(see Table 1-1). Whereas in 1960 the husband was the only wage
earner in 57 percent of all husband-wife families, by 1970 this was
true of only 47 percent of the families. Less than 50 percent of
married-couple families were supported solely by the husband for
the first time in 1967. In nearly 40 percent of families that year the
wife had worked, and in another 11 percent of families a member
other than the wife contributed to the support of the family. In 1976,
for the first time, half the wives were in the labor force at some time
during the year, and the proportion has increased since (see Table
1-5). The increase in the number of wage earners per family was
successful in the 1965 to 1969 period in offsetting the effects of the

Table 1-5 Distribution of Other Wage Earners in Husband-Wife Families: March 1959–1979 (percent)

Family Member(s) in Labor Force	1959	1960	1961	1962	1963	1964	1965
Total husband-wife families[a] (number in thousands)	34,625	35,041	35,453	35,713	36,079	36,286	36,545
Husband only	56.7	57.0	55.0	55.0	53.5	52.4	52.6
Wife or other member	43.3	43.0	45.0	45.0	46.5	47.6	47.4
Wife only	32.1	31.9	34.2	34.6	35.7	36.5	36.9
Other member only	11.2	11.1	10.8	10.4	10.8	11.1	10.5

	1966	1967	1968	1969	1970	1971	1972
Total husband-wife families (number in thousands)	36,763	37,060	37,668	38,144	38,639	38,496	39,116
Husband only	51.3	49.6	49.3	48.2	46.9	46.5	45.4
Wife or other member	48.7	50.4	50.7	51.8	53.1	53.5	54.6
Wife only	38.0	39.5	40.9	42.4	43.8	43.9	45.0
Other member only	10.7	10.9	9.8	9.4	9.3	9.6	9.6

	1973	1974	1975	1976	1977	1978	1979
Total husband-wife families (number in thousands)	39,298	39,312	39,173	39,026	39,093	38,824	38,970
Husband only	44.3	42.8	41.8	41.1	38.9	37.7	35.9
Wife or other member	55.7	57.2	58.2	58.9	61.1	62.3	64.0
Wife only	45.8	47.4	49.0	50.0	52.0	53.5	55.5
Other member only	9.9	9.8	9.2	8.9	9.1	8.8	8.5

SOURCE: U.S. Department of Labor, Bureau of Labor Statistics, *Handbook of Labor Statistics*, December 1980, Table 58.
[a] Families in which husband is in the labor force. Married couples living in households in which a relative is the householder are excluded. Hence the number of husband-wife families reported here is smaller than the number of married couples in which both spouses are present.

decline in real wages. Median family income increased 35.4 percent between 1960 and 1969, rising from $6,347 in 1960 to $7,355 in 1965 and $8,598 in 1969, all measured in constant (1967) dollars.[36]

Despite the continued increase in the number of wives in the labor force and in the number of two-earner families, median family income fell in both 1970 and 1971 as a result of the recession. Thus the new decade got off to a slow start, and its economic record did not improve. Inflation, recession, and slow productivity growth all marked the decade of the 1970s and took their toll on family income. After increases in excess of 35 percent in each of the preceding decades, median family income increased only 6.5 percent between 1970 and 1978.[37] This leveling off of real income occurred despite the continuing increase in the number of families with two or more wage earners. After 1970 this increase in families with more than one wage earner was able to do little more than keep real family income from declining. Real spendable wages of a worker with three dependents, meanwhile, rose from $90.20 in 1970 to $97.11 in 1972 before declining precipitously to $90.35 in 1975. By 1979 real wages had fallen below their 1970 level and were $89.49, and in October 1980 they stood at $83.34.[38]

In families in which the wife was employed, her earnings accounted for slightly more than 26 percent of family income in 1970, 1975, and 1977. The percentage was even higher among younger married couples. When the wife worked full time, she earned a median of $8,600 and contributed more than 38 percent of the family's total income in 1977 (see Table 1-6). Median family income of families in which the wife was in the paid labor force was substantially higher in the 1970s than that of families in which the wife was a full-time homemaker. The ratio of median family income of married-couple families in which the wife had a job to that of families in which she did not was 1.35 (see Table 1-7 on page 30).

In the context of a declining real wage, the family of a married woman who left the labor force would suffer an immediate and substantial reduction in real income, with little hope of making it up through an offsetting increase in the husband's earnings. A middle-income family could expect a decline in its income status if the wife stopped working. Thus the primary motive behind the more continuous pattern of employment for women and the dramatic increase in labor force participation rates of young married women with preschool children is straightforward enough: Their families depended on their earnings and would have suffered a large

Table 1-6 Contribution of Wife's Earnings to Total Family Income for Married-Couple Families,[a] by Selected Characteristics, 1970, 1975, 1977

	Median Percentage of Family Income Accounted for by Wife's Earnings		
Characteristic	1970	1975	1977
Total wives with work experience	26.7	26.3	26.1
Age of husband			
Under 25 years	30.2	30.7	28.9
25 years and over	26.3	25.9	25.8
Work experience of wife			
Worked 50 to 52 weeks full-time	38.6	38.8	38.2
Worked 27 to 49 weeks full-time	29.7	30.7	29.8
Worked 1 to 26 weeks full-time or 1 to 52 weeks part-time	11.9	11.8	11.1

SOURCE: U.S. Department of Commerce, Bureau of the Census, Current Population Reports, Series P-23, No. 100, February 1980, Table 9-7.
[a] Data include only those families in which the wife had paid work experience.

and irrevocable decline in living standards had they left paid employment for full-time homemaking. Their contribution to family income in the 1970s was indispensable.

In a sense, the increase in the number of families in which both husband and wife worked blunted the effect of the decline in real spendable wages. After 1967 husband-wife families in which the husband worked typically had more than one wage earner, and after 1976 both husband and wife were in the labor force in more than half the families (see Table 1-5). Perversely, the rationale used to pay women wages equal to 60 percent of those paid to men, on the assumption that most women were dependent on husbands for part of their support, now appears to justify payment of lower real wages to men on the assumption that most of them have wives contributing (or able to contribute) to the family's income. As a result, necessity forces more and more married women to seek paid employment and to remain gainfully employed for most of their married lives.

Continued growth of employment in the feminized sectors of the economy provided women with job opportunities throughout the 1970s. The number of women workers continued to increase by more than a million a year in every year between 1971 and 1979.[39] Despite the deep recession of 1973–1975 and the general economic malaise that characterized the decade, employment expanded at a

Table 1-7 Median Income of Married-Couple Families, by Type of Family, in 1970, 1975, 1977 (in 1977 Dollars)

Type of Family	1970		1975		1977	
	Number	*Median Income*	*Number*	*Median Income*	*Number*	*Median Income*
Median Family Income:						
Married-couple family	44,739	$16,411	47,318	$16,739	47,385	$17,616
Wife in paid labor force	17,568	19,158	20,833	19,408	21,936	20,268
Wife not in paid labor force	27,172	14,520	16,486	14,358	25,449	15,063
Ratio of Median Family Income:						
Wife in paid labor force/wife not in paid labor force	0.65	1.32	0.79	1.35	0.86	1.35

SOURCE: U.S. Department of Commerce, Bureau of the Census, Current Population Reports, Series P-23, No. 100, February 1980, Table 9-8.

startling rate. A comparison of the pre- and post-recession years 1972 and 1978 indicates that 12.7 million new jobs were created during that period. As in the previous two decades, clerical and service occupations provided much of the new employment, accounting for 2.7 million new clerical jobs and 2.1 million new service jobs. Of the 7.8 million women who joined the ranks of employed workers between 1972 and 1978, 4.1 million were hired for clerical and service jobs. Another million found jobs in sales or as registered nurses or health technicians.[40]

Though much of the employment growth in the 1970s was in the feminized sector of the economy, and women continued to be recruited for these "female" jobs, changes in the legal environment and women's struggles for equal treatment at work and for access to nontraditional jobs yielded some encouraging developments. Between 1972 and 1978, 2.1 million positions as managers and administrators were added. About 950,000 of these new jobs were filled by women. As a result, the ratio of women to men in this occupational category increased from 0.21 in 1972 to 0.30 in 1978. A positive, if modest, gain in employment in craft occupations can also be observed. More than 300,000 women were hired as craft workers during this period, though the effect on the ratio of women to men in the occupation—an increase from 0.04 to 0.06—was negligible.[41]

Changing Employment Patterns and Sex Roles

Continued expansion during the 1970s of the kinds of paid work that women do, together with the reduction in real wages over this period and the decline in economic security of families associated with three recessions (1969–1970, 1973–1975, and 1980) in little more than a decade, engendered a change in life-cycle employment patterns of a substantial number of women. The changes include a more continuous attachment to the labor force, the postponement of childbearing until a career or seniority rights are established, a shorter period of withdrawal from paid employment when children are born, and increased labor force participation while children are young. If not reversed in the 1980s, these changes may prove to have profound implications for the relationship between men and women as the major division of labor between the sexes will no longer be associated with paid employment outside the home for men and unpaid domestic labor for women. Traditional sex roles within the family and occupational segregation within the labor mar-

ket both presuppose a dominant role for men and a subordinate role
for women. Both also rely on the economic dependence of women
on their husbands, especially while their children are young, to
enforce second-class status for women. Recent economic developments, changes in the legal environment, and trends in women's
labor force participation patterns in the last decade have combined
to undermine these assumptions. Acknowledgment of the new reality that many married-couple families also depend on the wife's
paycheck for economic survival may be a step toward greater
equality between men and women in marriage.

Full equality in social relations between men and women, however, requires that status and income differentials based on sex be
eliminated in the labor market. The possibilities for accomplishing
this are related to the expansion of the economy with its attendant
opening up of opportunities for employment and advancement, and
its relative affluence and relaxation of social pressures for confor-
mity. Conversely, economic recession and retrenchment inhibit the
progress of women toward full equality. Increasing competition for
scarce jobs undermines affirmative action policies and nullifies recent gains through the operation of seniority provisions that run
counter to the interests of newly hired women workers. Generally,
the effect of slow growth or recession is to reduce women's aspirations and to force women into a struggle just to hold on to the
clerical, sales, and service jobs they have. In a shrinking job market,
in which employment is not keeping pace with population, it is
possible to anticipate a resurgence of traditional ideas about "wom-
en's place." The danger is that such a resurgence of traditional views
about appropriate socioeconomic roles for women will provide the
ideological basis for maintaining women in the labor force on the old
terms. Rigid sexual stereotypes in the labor market translate into the
further crowding of women in the "feminized sectors" and continued
disparities in earnings between men and women. For women, the
problems that emerge during periods of slow economic growth are
likely to be compounded in the remaining decades of this century by
a secular slowdown in the growth of "women's" jobs. New techniques of information storage, transmission, and retrieval, and the
advent of the "paperless" office, expected in the 1980s, will have a
negative impact on the demand for clerical workers. A declining
school age population has already reduced opportunities in teaching,
traditionally a female profession; and proposed cutbacks in public

expenditures for health care may reduce opportunities for women as nurses, health technicians, or health service workers.

The relative difficulty or ease with which women enter occupations currently dominated by men, their success in obtaining equal access to job training and advancement opportunities, and their success in establishing the principle that women should be compensated at the same rate as men for comparable work are, therefore, related to the more general questions of achieving economic growth and full employment. The full integration of women into the economic life of American society cannot be divorced from the broader economic issues of our times.

Patterns of Labor Force Participation of Women: Some Consequences

By 1967 nearly half the married women with school age children were in the labor force, as were about a quarter of those with children under six years old. Two distinct patterns of labor force participation over the life cycle for women who assume the roles of wife, mother, and worker were by that year readily observable. The first pattern, which emerged in the 1950s and is still followed by many women today, is one in which married women withdraw entirely from the work force some time after marriage to engage full time in household and other unpaid work, returning at some later date to full-time or part-time employment. Considerable variation occurs in the timing of such withdrawals and of subsequent re-entry into the labor force, and hence there are substantial differences in the length of the period during which a woman is out of the labor force. However, the longest period of withdrawal generally takes place following the birth of the first child, with re-entry commonly occurring when the youngest child enters school. The second pattern, which emerged in the mid-sixties and became increasingly important throughout the 1970s, is one in which women withdraw from the labor force only briefly, or perhaps not at all, following marriage and/or the birth of their first child. Both of these patterns represent a break with the pattern of female employment that prevailed in the half century prior to World War II when the female labor force consisted almost entirely of single women, and paid work was generally viewed as the stage in the female life cycle between leaving school and marriage. As a result of these shifts, well over half of all women 30 to 44 years of age are now in the labor force.[42] Thus many women have undertaken the difficult task of combining family responsibilities with paid work outside the home and are confronted with the necessity of allocating time and energy between household and job. Despite these conflicting demands, an increasing number of women have made a more permanent commitment to market work and seek a more continuous pattern of labor force participation. Nevertheless, for many women, career discontinuity—withdrawing from and then re-entering the labor force—remains a necessary accommodation to competing demands on their time.

In the early years of marriage, then, some women withdraw from paid employment for an extended period while household and family responsibilities are heaviest. Others, however, pursue a more continuous pattern of labor force participation, withdrawing only briefly or not at all when their children are young. The pattern followed is likely to have important consequences for the employment and earnings experiences of these women in subsequent periods of their lives. Yet comparatively little is known about the consequences to a woman of withdrawing from the labor force for a protracted period of time. The National Longitudinal Survey of Mature Women, a study of 5,000 women between the ages of 30 and 44 in 1967 when the first survey was conducted, who were surveyed six additional times through 1976, provides a data set that is especially well suited to an examination of the consequences to women of leaving the paid labor force to engage full time in unpaid domestic service at home. It is possible, using this data set, to identify two groups of women, one following the pattern of lengthy withdrawal at the time the first child is born and the other following a more continuous employment pattern. The procedure for selecting these two samples of women is discussed in Chapter 2. The samples are then utilized to explore several substantive issues.

In Chapter 3, the economic costs to women of a lengthy withdrawal rather than more continuous employment are investigated. The earnings of women with a discontinuous work history are compared with those of women who were employed more continuously. Techniques developed in the literature on sex discrimination in earnings are utilized to decompose the wage differential between these women into two parts—one reflecting differences in work-related characteristics and the other reflecting differential treatment by employers.

In the fourth chapter these two groups of women are again compared, but it is differences in the rewards *from* work (job satisfaction) rather than the rewards *for* work (hourly earnings) that are investigated. Women who follow one or the other of these employment patterns may differ from each other in (1) the satisfaction they derive from market work and homemaking and/or (2) their ability to reconcile competing demands on their time and energy from home and work. We expect, therefore, to find important differences in the factors that contribute to the job satisfaction of these two groups of women. The probit model, rather than ordinary least squares, is appropriate for analyzing the factors influencing job satisfaction and is utilized here.

The fifth chapter investigates the experiences of women who are returning to employment at part-time or full-time jobs after a lengthy absence from the labor force. Women who are re-entering the labor force after having dropped out entirely for a period of time experience varying degrees of success in making this transition. Three measures of successful work experience—hourly earnings, prestige, and job satisfaction—are examined. The impact on these measures of success of a host of non-home, non-market activities in which women engage is analyzed. These activities include preparation for a career (high school curriculum, college major, learning shorthand and typing), post-school investments in human capital (returning to school, completing a training program), and characteristics of jobs held early in the career.

Chapter 6 addresses the issues involved in returning to the labor force as a part-time worker rather than seeking full-time employment. The well-known fact that average wages of part-time workers are lower than those of full-time workers suggests that there may be negative consequences for women in resolving conflicting demands on their time by accepting part-time work. This chapter explores the extent of these effects and investigates the impact of differences in education or work experience on the wages of part-time workers.

The final chapter considers the prospects for continued rapid increases in the labor force participation of married women in the next decade.

Endnotes

1. For a fuller discussion of occupational segregation by sex, see Nancy S. Barrett, "Women in the Job Market: Occupations, Earnings and Career Opportunities," in Ralph E. Smith, ed., *The Subtle Revolution: Women at Work* (Washington, D.C.: The Urban Institute, 1979).

2. U.S. Department of Commerce, Bureau of the Census, *Statistical Abstract of the United States: 1974*, Table 550.

3. This argument is developed at length in Valerie Kincade Oppenheimer, *The Female Labor Force in the United States: Demographic and Economic Factors Governing Its Growth and Changing Composition* (Berkeley: University of California, 1970).

4. U.S. Department of Labor, Bureau of Labor Statistics, *Handbook of Labor Statistics* (December 1980), Table 4.

5. U.S. Department of Labor, Bureau of Labor Statistics, *Length of Working Life for Men and Women, 1970*, Special Labor Force Report No. 187 (1977).

6. This result is reported in Karen Oppenheim Mason, John L. Czajka, and Sara Arber, "Changes in U.S. Women's Sex-Role Attitudes, 1964–1974," *American Sociological Review*, 4 (August 1976), pp. 573–596. The authors found that 54 percent of women surveyed in 1964 agreed with this statement, but by 1970 the percentage with this view had increased to 73 percent. Attitudes prevailing in the 1930s are reported in Oppenheimer, *op. cit.* See also Hazel Erskine, "The Polls: Women's Role," *Public Opinion Quarterly*, 35 (Summer 1971), pp. 282–284.

7. Karen Oppenheim Mason and Larry L. Bumpass, "U.S. Women's Sex Role Ideology, 1970," *American Journal of Sociology*, 80 (March 1975), pp. 1212–1219.

8. Kathryn E. Walker and Margaret E. Woods, *Time Use: A Measure of House-hold Production of Family Goods and Services* (American Home Economics Association, 1976). Cited in Clair Vickery, "Women's Economic Contribution to the Family" in Ralph E. Smith, ed., *The Subtle Revolution: Women at Work* (Washington, D.C.: The Urban Institute, 1979). Also, the Michigan Survey Research Center (SRC) survey of time use in the United States in 1965 confirms this finding. A later SRC survey, conducted with a small sample in 1975, indicates there may have been a change in these patterns, with women spending less time in housework. The SRC finding is that married women spent 239 minutes a day in housework in 1975 compared with 265 minutes in 1965; married women who work spent 143 minutes a day in housework in 1975 compared with 181 in 1965. Married men spent 95 minutes in housework in 1975 compared with 97 in 1965. The SRC survey found that full sharing of responsiblities was rare. These results are reported in Frank P. Stafford, "Women's Use of Time Converging with Men's," *Monthly Labor Review*, 103 (December 1980), pp. 57–59.

9. Walker and Woods, *op. cit.*

10. Cited in Barrett, *op. cit.*

11. For a discussion of labor market segmentation and its historical development, see Richard Edwards, *Contested Terrain: The Transformation of the Workplace in the Twentieth Century* (New York: Basic Books, Inc., 1979).

12. U.S. Department of Labor, Bureau of Labor Statistics, *Handbook of Labor Statistics* (December 1980), Table 3.

13. U.S. Department of Commerce, Bureau of the Census, *Current Population Reports*, Series P-23, No. 100 (February 1980), Table 9-7.

14. U.S. Department of Health, Education and Welfare, Public Health Service, "100 Years of Marriage and Divorce Statistics, United States, 1867–1967," *Vital Health Statistics*, Series 21, No. 24 (December 1973).

15. Discussed in Sandra L. Hofferth and Kristin A. Moore, "Women's Employment and Marriage" in Ralph E. Smith, ed., *The Subtle Revolution: Women at Work* (Washington, D.C.: The Urban Institute, 1979).

16. Vickery, *op. cit.*

17. U.S. Department of Labor, Bureau of Labor Statistics, *Handbook of Labor Statistics* (December 1980), Table 96. The figures refer to spendable average weekly earnings of production or nonsupervisory workers on private nonagricultural payrolls in constant (1967) dollars.

18. U.S. Department of Commerce, Bureau of the Census, *Historical Statistics of the United States: Colonial Times to 1970*, Series G189-204.

19. Article 213 of the Economy Act of 1932 required that persons living with a spouse also employed by the government be discharged first when government employees were laid off. This was interpreted to mean that married women workers with husbands who were also government employees should be dismissed.

20. U.S. Department of Commerce, Bureau of the Census, *Current Population Reports*, Series P-23, No. 100 (February 1980), Table 3-1.

21. *Ibid.*, Table 3-2.

22. Elizabeth Waldman, Allyson Sherman Grossman, Howard Hayghe, and Beverly L. Johnson, "Working Mothers in the 1970's: A Look at the Statistics," *Monthly Labor Review*, 102 (October 1979), pp. 39–49.

23. Beverly L. Johnson, "Marital and Family Characteristics of Workers, 1970–1978," *Monthly Labor Review*, 102 (April 1979), pp. 49–52.

24. Waldman *et al.*, *op. cit.*

25. U.S. Department of Commerce, Bureau of the Census, *Current Population Reports*, Series P-23, No. 100 (February 1980), Table 3-1.

26. Paul C. Glick, "Updating the Life Cycle of the Family," *Journal of Marriage and the Family*, 39 (February 1977), pp. 3–15.

27. U.S. Department of Commerce, Bureau of the Census, *Current Population Reports*, Series P-23, No. 100 (February 1980), Table 3-2.

28. Glick, *op. cit.*

29. Waldman *et al.*, *op. cit.*

30. Mary Jo Bane, *Here to Stay: American Families in the Twentieth Century* (New York: Basic Books, Inc., 1976).

31. U.S. Department of Labor, Women's Bureau, *20 Facts on Women Workers* (December 1980).

32. Two recent studies found that only about 25 percent of the increase in female labor force participation in this period was due to shifts among family-characteristic groups. The major share of the increase, according to these studies, resulted from increase in participation within family-characteristic groups. See George L. Perry, "Potential Output and Productivity," *Brookings Papers on Economic Activity* (1977:1), pp. 11–60, and Ralph E. Smith, "Sources

of Growth of the Female Labor Force, 1971–75," *Monthly Labor Review*, 100 (August 1977), pp. 27–29.

33. U.S. Department of Labor, Bureau of Labor Statistics, *Perspectives on Working Women: A Databook*, Bulletin 2080 (October 1980), Table 28. Refers to March 1979.

34. U.S. Department of Labor, Women's Bureau, *20 Facts on Women Workers* (December 1980).

35. U.S. Department of Labor, Bureau of Labor Statistics, *Handbook of Labor Statistics* (December 1980), Table 96.

36. U.S. Department of Commerce, Bureau of the Census, *Historical Statistics of the United States: Colonial Times to 1970*, Series G189-204.

37. U.S. Department of Commerce, Bureau of the Census, *Current Population Reports*, Series P-60, No. 118 (March 1979), Table C, and *Current Population Reports*, Series P-60, No. 123 (March 1980), Table A.

38. U.S. Department of Labor Statistics, *Handbook of Labor Statistics* (December 1980), Table 96; and U.S. Department of Labor, Bureau of Labor Statistics, *Employment and Earnings* (December 1980), Table C-5.

39. U.S. Department of Labor, Bureau of Labor Statistics, *Handbook of Labor Statistics* (December 1980), Table 3.

40. U.S. Department of Commerce, Bureau of the Census, *Current Population Reports*, Series P-23, No. 100 (February 1980), Table 8-1.

41. *Ibid.*

42. Robert W. Bednarzik and Deborah P. Klein, *Labor Force Trends: A Synthesis and Analysis*, U.S. Department of Labor, Bureau of Labor Statistics, Special Labor Force Report 208 (1977).

Chapter 2

SELECTION OF
THE SAMPLES

The data for this study are from the National Longitudinal Survey (NLS) of Mature Women. The NLS is a longitudinal study of about 5,000 women who were 30 to 44 years of age in 1967 when the first survey was conducted. These women constitute a representative national probability sample of the almost 18 million women in the United States non-institutionalized civilian population in this age cohort as of the first interview data. In order to provide a sufficient number of observations for reliable racial comparisons, the sampling ratio for black women was more than three times as high as for white women. As a result, the original sample of 5,083 women included 3,606 whites, 1,390 blacks, and 87 women of other races.[1] The samples were drawn and personal interviews were conducted by the U.S. Bureau of the Census for The Ohio State University Center for Human Resource Research under separate contracts with the U.S. Department of Labor.[2]

Stated succinctly, the NLS data include "an abbreviated lifetime work history of each respondent up to the time of the first survey, a detailed work history during the period covered by the surveys, and information about a variety of social, psychological, and economic characteristics of the respondents that are hypothesized to influence labor market behavior."[3] At the present time, data for this cohort of women are available for public use from the interviews conducted in 1967, 1968 (mail), 1969, 1971, 1972, 1974 (telephone), and 1976 (telephone).

The cohort of women 30 to 44 years of age in 1967 is especially appropriate for the study of the issues involved in the successful integration of mature women into the work force. Indeed, this cohort of women was selected for inclusion in the NLS precisely because in the past several decades so many married women have re-entered the labor force during this period of their lives.[4] Moreover, the NLS, because it is longitudinal and comprises a national sample, provides one of the few data bases that can be used to analyze these issues.

The Two Samples to Be Analyzed

To explore the issues raised above, two samples of working women were selected from the National Longitudinal Survey of Mature Women. The women in both samples followed similar life-cycle patterns: leaving school (though many returned to school later), working full-time for a while, marrying and then bearing (or assuming responsibility for) one or more children.* Their work patterns, however, differed. The women in the first sample left the labor force following either marriage or the birth of their first child and did not return to paid employment for at least three years. The average length of absence from the labor force for women in this group was 11.7 years. The women in the second sample stopped working for less than three years following marriage or the assumption of responsibility for their first child. The women included in both samples were further constrained to have some paid employment in the years between 1967 and 1976, though continuous employment during that period in the years following re-entry was not a condition for selection into either sample. In addition, the women included in this study are white. For, despite the fact that black women were oversampled in the NLS by a ratio of approximately three to one, very few of the black women interviewed followed the first employment pattern.† The phenomenon of married women withdrawing entirely

---

* The women included in the two samples had their first child by 1967. Very few women could be identified who followed this life cycle pattern, but did not bear or assume responsibility for a child by that date. Several of these women acquired children who were already of school age. Incomplete data existed for several others. Still others left the labor force after first assuming responsibility for a child and had not returned to work by 1972 or 1976. At most, a small number of women who had their first child after 1967 could have been included in the analysis. Limited resources precluded this possibility.

† Only 102 black women followed the first employment pattern, withdrawing from the labor force for three or more years and then returning to paid employment. Of these, only 65 were in the labor force in 1972 and 68 in 1976.

from the labor force some time after marriage to engage full time in household and other non-paid tasks, returning to work after a long absence, occurs almost entirely among white women. This is not true, it should be noted, of the second employment pattern. As expected on the basis of the sampling design of the NLS, nearly 33 percent of the women who followed the second pattern are black. Unfortunately, the small number of black women who followed the first pattern is insufficient to permit a separate analysis of the issues considered here for black women, and we must reluctantly limit the analysis in this volume to white women.[5]

The sample sizes for the two groups of women actually analyzed in this volume vary from chapter to chapter for several reasons. The evaluation of the economic costs of withdrawing from paid employment in Chapter 3 requires that the women included in the analysis have hourly earnings in 1972 and/or 1976. Sample size in Chapter 4 is affected by the fact that the questions on job satisfaction and husband's approval were last asked in 1972. The samples must be restricted in this chapter to married women, husbands present, who were employed in 1972 so that the effects of the husband's attitude toward the employment of his wife on the wife's job satisfaction can be analyzed. Again, in Chapter 5, it was necessary to constrain the sample to include women with jobs in 1972 and/or 1976.

Comparison of Personal and Work Experience Characteristics

Since both groups of women followed the same life-cycle pattern (though not the same employment patterns), it is not surprising that the profiles of their personal and family characteristics (that is, father's education, own education, health status, presence of children under the age of 18, region of residence, and size of the local labor force in region of residence) presented in Table 2-1 are so similar. The only unanticipated difference between the two groups of women is that a smaller proportion of the husbands of women who withdrew for three or more years earned more than $10,000. The other difference, in age of young children, is a consequence of the fact that the average length of time out of the labor force for women who withdrew for three or more years was 11.7 years. Younger women who are following this employment pattern may not have returned to work by 1972. It may also be of interest to note that

Table 2-1   Profile of Selected Personal and Family Characteristics, 1972

Characteristics	Ever-Married White Women with Children Gap ≥ 3	Ever-Married White Women with Children Gap < 3
Proportion whose father's education ≥ 10 years	0.25	0.24
Average number of years of schooling	11.68 years	11.95 years
Proportion who are in their late 30s	0.22	0.35
Proportion who are in their early 40s	0.31	0.33
Proportion who are in their late 40s	0.47	0.32
Proportion who are in good health	0.89	0.90
Proportion who reside in the South	0.22	0.24
Proportion living in areas where the local labor force numbers 300,000 or less	0.61	0.68
Proportion who have child < 6 years old	0.05	0.12
Proportion with no children at home 17 or younger	0.12	0.13
Proportion currently married, husband present	0.84	0.82
Proportion with husbands who earn more than $10,000	0.35	0.42
Proportion of currently married women whose husbands strongly approve of their working	0.28	0.28
Proportion of currently married women who strongly approve of mothers of young children working	0.36	0.45

similar proportions of both groups of women report that their husbands strongly approve of their working. Not surprisingly, a somewhat smaller proportion of the women who did not work for many years after assuming homemaking and child-rearing responsibilities strongly approved of the mothers of young children working.

Average values of the work experience variables are presented in Table 2-2. The average number of weeks worked between 1968 and 1972 is about the same for both groups, though, of course, the average number of years through 1967 in which six or more months

Table 2-2   Mean Values of Selected Work Experience Characteristics, 1972

Characteristics	Ever-Married White Women with Children Gap ≥ 3	Ever-Married White Women with Children Gap < 3
Number of years worked 6 or more months by 1967	8.5 years	12.4 years
Number of weeks worked between 1968 and 1972	168 weeks	173 weeks
Tenure on current job (years)	4.7 years	5.6 years
Proportion who have jobs that are covered by union contract	0.20	0.16
Proportion who work full time, 35 hours or more	0.69	0.75
Proportion employed in professional, technical, or managerial occupations	0.16	0.25
Proportion employed in clerical occupations	0.45	0.41
Proportion employed in all other civilian occupations	0.39	0.34
Proportion employed in manufacturing, mining, and construction industries	0.27	0.23
Proportion employed in wholesale and retail trade	0.20	0.18
Proportion employed in public utilities, finance, insurance, and real estate	0.17	0.20
Proportion employed in professional service	0.32	0.34
Proportion employed in other service industries	0.04	0.05
Hourly earnings	$2.75	$3.07
Social status of the job (Bose index)	46.98	49.38

were worked is smaller for the group that had the lengthy absence. Women in this group also had less tenure in their current job, were less likely to work full time, and were more likely to be in jobs covered by a union contract. Both hourly wages and social status of the job were lower for women who left the labor force for a protracted period when they assumed marital and/or child care responsibilities than for those whose absence was shorter. Important differences between these two groups of women can also be observed in the occupations, and to a lesser extent in the industries, in which the jobs they held are located.

Endnotes

1. Carol L. Jusenius and Herbert S. Parnes, "Introduction and Overview" in Herbert S. Parnes *et al.*, *Dual Careers: A Longitudinal Analysis of the Labor Market Experience of Women*, Vol. 4, U.S. Department of Labor (Washington, D.C.: U.S. Government Printing Office, 1975).
2. For an overview of the entire NLS data base, including a complete description of the sampling design, interviewing procedures, and included variables see the *National Longitudinal Surveys Handbook* (Columbus, Ohio: Center for Human Resources Research, Ohio State University, 1977). The cohort of mature women is described at length in Herbert S. Parnes, John R. Shea, Ruth S. Spitz, and Fredrich A. Zeller, *Dual Careers: A Longitudal Analysis of the Labor Market Experience of Women*, Vol. 1, U.S. Department of Labor (Washington, D.C.: U.S. Government Printing Office, 1970), Chapter 1.
3. Jusenius and Parnes, *op. cit.*, p. 5.
4. Parnes, Shea, Spitz, and Zeller, *op. cit.*, preface.
5. Prior research with the NLS suggests that it is inappropriate to analyze a combined sample of black and white women with a dummy variable to capture the effects of race. Such models are seriously misspecified. See Barbara A. Jones, "Introductory Remarks" in *Women's Changing Roles at Home and on the Job*, National Commission for Manpower Policy, Special Report No. 26 (Washington, D.C.: U.S. Government Printing Office, September 1978).

Chapter 3

THE ECONOMIC COSTS OF DROPPING OUT

As we saw in Chapter 2, married white women with children confront a complex issue at the point in their lives at which they first assume responsibility for a child: whether to withdraw completely from the labor force for several years or more while rearing the child (and any subsequent children), or whether to return to work after a shorter absence. Many considerations enter into this decision. Some are related to beliefs about child rearing or about the appropriate division of labor between husband and wife. Others are related to the inadequacy of available support systems for working mothers—for example, the national shortage of day-care facilities for preschool age children and of after-school programs for older children, and the complete absence of infirmaries or other facilities for sick-child care while the mother works. Economic factors, too, enter into this decision. It is usually a straightforward matter for a woman with prior work experience to calculate the income she will forego during her absence from paid employment. The Commission on Population Growth and the American Future estimated that in 1977 the earnings foregone by a mother staying out of the labor force until her child reached 14 years of age amounted to $75,000 for a woman with an elementary school education and $155,000 for a woman with a postgraduate college education. The average woman could expect to give up $100,000 of earnings.[1] Great as these costs are, however, they may not measure the total economic cost to her of dropping out of the paid work force. Hourly earnings and/or prestige status of jobs held after re-entry may be substantially lower for women who do not work for a prolonged period than for women with a more continuous work history. If this is, in fact, the case, the costs of dropping out will be considerably in excess of the initial income foregone. This chapter examines the effect of a protracted withdrawal from the labor force on hourly earnings and job status in subsequent periods. Women are viewed as having been out of the labor force for a prolonged period if they left for three or more years. The average length of absence for women in this group is 11.7 years.

Prestige Status of Later Jobs

The last year for which an appropriate measure for women of the prestige status of the job held[2] is available in the data set is 1972. The average prestige status of the 1972 job (or, if the woman is not currently employed, of the most recent job held since 1967) can be compared with the average prestige status of the last job held prior to assuming responsibility for a child for the first time. The comparison is made for both groups of women in order to assess the effects of dropping out of paid employment on job status. The prestige status of the last job held prior to the assumption of child care responsibilities is the same for both groups of women—46.8 for women with a more continuous employment pattern, 46.6 for those with a more discontinuous employment pattern. Comparing current or last job with this earlier job, it can be seen that average prestige status declined slightly to 45.5 for women who withdrew for three or more years, while increasing slightly to 47.5 for women who withdrew for a shorter period. The resulting difference between the two groups of women in average prestige status of most recent job is only two points. Of course, the prestige status of current or last job may refer to a job held as far back as 1967 for a woman who is not working in 1972. Differences between the two groups of women in the proportion employed in 1972 may affect the observed difference in prestige status. If, for this reason, we restrict the comparison to those who were employed in 1972, the scores are 47.0 and 49.4 respectively—a difference still of only 2.4 points.

The small differential in average prestige scores does not tell the whole story, however. Higher standard deviations are associated with the mean values of prestige status for women who withdrew for less than three years. This implies greater variation in prestige scores for women in this group. That is, while the means for the two groups are similar, this group may have both more women with high prestige scores and more with low. In addition, there may be differences between the two groups of women in the proportions whose prestige scores move up, move down, or stay the same. These issues are explored in Table 3-1. The comparison here is limited to women in both groups who were employed in 1972. This avoids the ambiguity of measuring recent prestige status for some women in 1972 and for others in earlier years. Prestige status scores for the two groups of women ranged from a low of 11 to a high of 88. The scores were divided into "high" (70 or better), "medium high" (50 to 69),

Table 3-1 Comparison of Prestige Status of 1972 Job with Prestige Status of Last Job Held Prior to Assuming Responsibility for First Child

White Women, Gap ≥ 3 Years

	Prestige Status Last Job before Child				
Prestige Status 1972 Job	High Number (Percent)	Medium High Number (Percent)	Medium Low Number (Percent)	Low Number (Percent)	Total (Percent)
High	13	11	5	1	30
	(61.9)	(4.3)	(2.9)	(2.1)	(6.0)
Medium High	6	167	49	9	231
	(28.6)	(65.2)	(28.0)	(18.8)	(46.2)
Medium Low	2	66	95	20	183
	(9.5)	(25.8)	(54.3)	(41.7)	(36.6)
Low	0	12	26	18	56
	(0)	(4.7)	(14.9)	(37.5)	(11.2)

N = 500

White Women, Gap < 3 Years

	Prestige Status Last Job before Child				
Prestige Status 1972 Job	High Number (Percent)	Medium High Number (Percent)	Medium Low Number (Percent)	Low Number (Percent)	Total (Percent)
High	13	12	2	1	28
	(81.3)	(7.5)	(2.0)	(2.9)	(9.0)
Medium High	3	112	37	9	161
	(18.8)	(69.6)	(37.4)	(26.5)	(51.9)
Medium Low	0	30	46	10	86
	(0)	(18.6)	(46.5)	(29.4)	(27.7)
Low	0	7	14	14	35
	(0)	(4.3)	(14.1)	(41.2)	(11.3)

N = 309

"medium low" (30 to 49), and "low" (29 or less). Cross-tabulations of prestige status of 1972 job by prestige status of last job held prior to having the first child are presented for both groups of women.

The tabulations in Table 3-1 indicate considerably more movement than was suggested by the small changes in the mean values of the prestige scores. A comparison of the two groups of women indicates that a higher proportion of those who worked more continuously moved into higher prestige jobs (22.9 percent as compared with 19.0 percent) while a smaller proportion moved into lower prestige jobs (17.4 percent as compared with 22.4 percent). Most women, nevertheless, experience no prestige changes sufficient to move them to another category. Among women who were out of the labor force for three or more years, 58.6 percent held jobs in 1972 in the same prestige category as the job they held before dropping out. For those who worked more continuously, a similar proportion (59.7 percent) experienced no change in prestige category. This similarity is tempered, however, by the fact that a larger proportion of women in this latter group held high status jobs initially.

Despite the small differences in the *mean* values of prestige status of the job, women who work more continuously tend to obtain more prestigious jobs. A higher proportion of these women move from medium low status in the last job before children to medium high status in the 1972 job, or from medium high status in the last job before children to high status in the 1972 job. Moreover, 81 percent of women in high prestige jobs before they had children were still in high prestige jobs in 1972. For women who had previously held high status jobs but who dropped out for a protracted period, only 62 percent held high status jobs in 1972. Overall, in 1972, 61 percent of the women who worked more continuously held high or medium high status jobs while only 52 percent of those with a more discontinuous work history held such jobs.

Thus women in medium high or medium low status jobs who drop out when they take on household and child-care tasks reduce the probability that they will hold more prestigious jobs later in their careers. Women in high status jobs increase the probability that they will experience a decline in prestige if they drop out. Only women in the lowest status jobs do not sacrifice gains in prestige by dropping out.

Effect on Hourly Earnings

The pattern of labor force participation may affect not only job status but hourly earnings as well. Average hourly earnings for the two groups of women can be compared in 1972 and again in 1976. The wages of women who returned to work after an absence of three or more years were, on the average, below those of women who worked more continuously in both years. In 1972 wages of women who had dropped out for three or more years were equal to 90 percent of the wages earned by women who worked more continuously. By 1976 the wage ratio had declined to 84 percent. In absolute terms, the wage gap between these two groups of women widened from 32 cents an hour to 64 cents an hour. Thus, in addition to the actual income foregone by women during the period in which they were absent from the labor force, a persistent and widening wage differential exists between these women and the women who left work for a shorter time.

There are two potential sources of this income differential. First, a lengthy absence following marriage or the birth of the first child results in fewer total years of work experience as well as a shorter period of tenure on the current job. Women in occupations in which employers provide firm-specific training, or in any occupation in which continuous employment results in the upgrading of skills, are likely to have fewer skills and to earn less if they have been out of the labor force for several years. Similarly, women who leave the labor force for a protracted period of time may find that the jobs available to them upon re-entry are in industries and/or occupations that traditionally require fewer skills, especially skills acquired on-the-job, and that pay less. Alternatively, it has been suggested that women generally are concentrated in occupations that neither reward them for work experience nor penalize them for having withdrawn from the labor force to fulfill family responsibilities.[3] If this is, in fact, the case, then differences in work experience will have a negligible effect on hourly earnings.

The second potential cause of lower wages for women returning to market work after a prolonged absence is that whatever their skills, experience, and other characteristics, employers will value and reward these characteristics differently than they would if there had been a short absence or none at all. This may occur because: (1) previously acquired skills may become obsolete or deteriorate rapidly during the extended period of disuse; (2) women who with-draw because of family responsibilities may seek less demanding jobs when re-entering employment and may not make use of the skills acquired earlier; and/or (3) employers may discriminate against women with a history of having withdrawn from the labor force, so that such women will not be hired for jobs requiring the previously learned skills.

The following procedure, originally proposed by Oaxaca[4] and widely used in the literature on male-female wage differentials,[5] allows the difference in average hourly earnings between women who withdrew from the labor force for three or more years and those who withdrew for a shorter period or not at all to be broken down into two components reflecting the two potential causes of reduced earnings described above. It seems reasonable to assume that the hourly earnings function (f_c) for the women with the more continu-ous work history would also be applicable to the women who were absent from the labor force for a prolonged period, if this latter group of women had also worked more continuously. In that case, we can estimate what the mean earnings for the women who dropped out would have been had they worked continuously by

$$\overline{D}_e = f_c(\overline{X}_i D)$$

where $\overline{D}_e$ represents estimated mean earnings, f_c represents the earnings function of women with a more continuous work history, and $\overline{X}_i D$ is a vector of the mean characteristic levels of the women who withdrew for a longer period of time. $\overline{D}_e$ represents the amount this latter group of women would have earned, with their own char-acteristics (for example, years of schooling, years of work experi-ence) unchanged, if they had been remunerated for these charac-teristics in the same way as were the women who worked more continuously.

The difference between actual average earnings of women who worked more continuously $(\overline{C})$ and actual average earnings of those who dropped out for a prolonged period $(\overline{D})$ can be decomposed as follows:

$\overline{C}-\overline{D}_e$ = the difference in mean earnings attributable to dif-ferences in the mean value of characteristics;

$\overline{D}_e-\overline{D}$ = the difference in mean earnings attributable to dif-ferences in the way in which the characteristics of the two groups are remunerated.

Table 3-2   **Decomposition of the Difference in Hourly Earnings between White Women with a More Continuous and Those with a More Discontinuous Work History**

	Employed, 1972	Employed, 1976	Employed, Both 1972 and 1976*
(1) Actual mean hourly earnings of women with a more continuous work history ($\overline{C}$)	$3.07	$4.11	$4.40
(2) Actual mean hourly earnings of women with a more discontinuous work history ($\overline{D}$)	2.75	3.47	3.67
(3) Actual earnings gap: $\overline{C} - \overline{D}$	0.32	0.64	0.73
(4) Estimated mean earnings of women with a more discontinuous work history ($\overline{D}_e$)	2.79	3.82	3.83
(5) Difference in mean earnings attributable to differences in the mean values of characteristics: $\overline{C} - \overline{D}_e$	0.28	0.30	0.57
(6) Difference in mean earnings attributable to differences in the way in which characteristics are remunerated: $\overline{D}_e - \overline{D}$	0.04	0.34	0.16

* Hourly earnings refer to 1976.

Thus we can use this decomposition to evaluate the importance of the two potential sources of reduced earnings to women who re-enter the labor force after an extended absence.

The results of that decomposition, presented in Table 3-2, show that while the differential in hourly earnings in 1972 was due almost entirely to differences between the two groups in qualifications, by 1976 these differences account for only half of the wage differential.* In 1972 nearly all of the wage gap between the two groups of women appears to be explained by differences in personal attributes, work-related characteristics (for example, usual hours worked, number of weeks worked between 1968 and 1972, and years through 1967 in which six or more months were worked), and industry and occupation variables. The residual wage gap after productivity differences are taken into consideration amounted to only 4 cents an hour, only 12.5 percent of the total differential. By 1976, however, slightly less than half the differential could be explained by differences in characteristics. The rest of the wage gap—amounting to about 34 cents an hour—is the result either of the women's unwillingness to pursue higher paying, more responsible jobs or, alternatively, of employers' unwillingness to consider women who have a history of having dropped out for the higher paying, more responsible jobs.

Thus differences in qualifications resulted in an hourly wage for women with a more discontinuous employment pattern that was 28 cents an hour lower in 1972 and 30 cents an hour lower in 1976 than the hourly wage of women who worked more continuously. Discrimination by employers against women who dropped out and/or reluctance by these women to accept more responsible jobs resulted in a residual difference in hourly wages of only 4 cents in 1972, but of 34 cents in 1976. This residual wage gap, unexplained by differences in either personal or work-related characteristics, amounted to more than 50 percent of the wage differential between the two groups of women in 1976.

Causes of the Increase in the Wage Gap

An important issue in evaluating the implications of this large increase in the size of the residual wage gap is whether it arises from the more limited opportunities for advancement and wage growth for women already employed in 1972 or whether it results from the hiring of women not employed in 1972 at wages that do not compensate them fully for their schooling, work experience, and other attributes. This issue is addressed in column 3 of Table 3-2, where the

---

* Means and coefficients of the wage equations used in carrying out the decomposition can be found in appendix tables A-1, A-2, and A-3.

wages of women with a more discontinuous work history who were employed in both 1972 and 1976 are compared with those of women with a more continuous work history who were also employed at both dates. As might be expected, average wages in 1976 were higher for women in both groups who were already employed in 1972. Comparing columns 2 and 3, it can be seen that the wage gap in absolute terms is also larger, although the ratio of wages paid to workers with a more discontinuous work pattern to those of workers with a more continuous pattern is unchanged at about 83 percent. The part of the wage gap that is unexplained by differences in characteristics has risen from 4 cents an hour in 1972 to 16 cents an hour in 1976. Thus the residual wage gap which amounted to 12.5 percent of the total differential in wages paid to these two groups of women in 1972 increased to 22 percent of the differential in 1976. This widening of the residual earnings gap suggests that the rate of earnings growth for women with a more discontinuous work history was slower than for women who worked more continuously. At the same time, it is also true that women who had left the work force for an extended period and who returned to work between 1972 and 1976 fared more poorly than those already employed in 1972. This is evident from the comparison of the wages of all women in each of the two groups (see column 2 of Table 3-2). As observed above, the residual wage gap when this comparison is made is 34 cents an hour—53 percent of the total differential between the two groups. There was thus a serious deterioration in the wage position of women returning to work between 1972 and 1976, after having dropped out for an extended period. The increase in the residual wage gap between 1972 and 1976, therefore, resulted from *both* lesser opportunities for subsequent advancement and wage growth for those women with discontinuous work histories who had re-entered the labor force by 1972 and from a serious deterioration in the ability of women returning after 1972 to translate their education, experience, and other attributes into appropriate wage levels.

Summary

The thrust of this chapter has been an investigation of the economic costs to women, in terms of prestige and hourly earnings, of dropping out of the work force for three or more years following marriage and the assumption of household and child care tasks. We found that for women in all but the lowest status jobs, dropping out of the labor force reduced the likelihood that the prestige score of the 1972 job would exceed the prestige score of the last job held prior to leaving paid employment. For women who held the highest status jobs, dropping out reduced the probability that the 1972 job would also be a high status job. Dropping out of the labor force also had a negative effect on hourly earnings, an effect that increased over the period 1972 to 1976. Whereas the wages in 1972 of women with a more discontinuous work history were 90 percent of those of women who had not withdrawn for an extended period following marriage or children, by 1976 they had declined to 84 percent. In 1972 nearly all of this differential could be attributed to differences in qualifications between the two groups of women: the residual wage gap was only 4 cents an hour. By 1976, however, the residual wage gap increased to 34 cents an hour when all women in each of the two groups are compared, and to 16 cents an hour when the comparison is restricted to women in each group who were employed in both 1972 and 1976. Both relatively and absolutely, the financial position of women who had withdrawn from the work force for a protracted period worsened.

Endnotes

1. Thomas J. Espenshade, "The Value and Costs of Children," *Population Bulletin*, 32 (Washington, D.C.: Population Reference Bureau, Inc., 1977), pp. 19–20.
2. C. Bose, "Women and Jobs: Sexual Influences on Occupational Prestige," Ph.D. dissertation, The Johns Hopkins University, 1973.
3. Harriet Zellner, "The Determinants of Occupational Segregation" in Cynthia B. Lloyd, ed., *Sex Discrimination and the Division of Labor* (New York: Columbia University Press, 1975).
4. Ronald L. Oaxaca, "Male-Female Wage Differentials in Urban Labor Markets," *International Economic Review*, 14 (October 1973), pp. 693–709.
5. See, for example, Alan Blinder, "Wage Discrimination: Reduced Form and Structural Estimates," *Journal of Human Resources*, 8 (Summer, 1973), pp. 436–455; and Brian Chiplin, "An Evaluation of Sex Discrimination" in Cynthia B. Lloyd, Emily S. Andrews, and Curtis L. Gilroy, eds., *Women in the Labor Market* (New York: Columbia University Press, 1979).

Chapter 4

JOB SATISFACTION OF
WORKING WIVES

The conflicts and role strains encountered by women who combine the traditional role of wife and mother with the role of wage earner have been acknowledged by researchers and commentators,[1] as have the attempts by some women to resolve these conflicts through part-time or intermittent employment at jobs located close to home.[2] Much less is known about the extent to which women have actually succeeded in resolving the conflicts they confront as they seek to meet the responsibilities of home and work. One of the few studies to address this question found that while more married women preferred part-time work to either full-time homemaking or full-time employment, women doing part-time work reported *lower* levels of satisfaction than women engaged in either of the other activities.[3] Some direct evidence on the extent of conflicts between work and family life for workers who are married or living with a child under eighteen is available in the 1977 Quality of Employment Survey.[4] Ten percent of the workers surveyed in that study reported severe conflicts between work and family life, while another 25 percent reported moderate conflicts. Parents experienced significantly more conflict than others. Surprisingly, almost equal proportions of employed husbands and employed wives reported severe or moderate conflict—34 percent of the husbands and 37 percent of the wives—although the ways in which work and family life conflict are different for men and women.* Employed women most commonly reported schedule conflicts or fatigue and irritability as the problem. Available energy for family life was a factor, especially for working wives with children. The study attributed this to women's greater family responsibilities.

Interaction Between Work Life and Home Life

The findings of the Quality of Employment Survey confirm that there are important connections between life at work and at home. It is not immediately clear, however, how marriage and employment interact to affect a woman's satisfaction with her life or her job. Investigators exploring the effects of working outside the home on the marital satisfaction of wives have come to contradictory conclusions. Studies can be cited in support of the view that working wives are less satisfied with their marriages than non-working wives, in support of the view that there are no differences in satisfaction, and in support of the view that working women are happier than non-working wives.[5] As Hofferth and Moore conclude in reviewing these studies, "It seems likely that a working/non-working dichotomy is too simplistic. Whether employment affects [marital] satisfaction depends upon various factors . . . ."[6] The factors mentioned include education, family income, wife's degree of work commitment, hours of work, and husband's attitude.

More agreement has emerged regarding the job satisfaction of working wives. Previous research appears to suggest that husband's disapproval and/or family responsibilities impose economic and psychic costs on women pursuing dual careers as wives and as workers that signficantly reduce the working wife's satisfaction with her job. In a study based on data from the 1972–1973 Quality of Employment Survey, Quinn *et al.*[7] found that working women with one or more children under the age of six in their households were appreciably less satisfied with their jobs than other women. The authors of that study speculated that women with preschoolers "may

---

* Though the proportions of men and women reporting conflict are about the same, the researchers suggest that the data may underestimate the amount of conflict women experience. Employed women may be less likely than men to acknowledge conflict because they feel others will use this as evidence that they should not be working. Moreover, married women with severe work-family conflicts may simply leave paid employment.

have poorer paying and otherwise less desirable jobs" and/or "the dual roles of worker and child-rearer may create problems relating to time, schedules, physical stamina, and payment for child care which are serious enough to decrease the attractiveness of jobs that women without (young) children might otherwise find satisfying."[8] Other researchers[9] have observed that many men do not have supportive attitudes toward their wives' employment, and that the husband's attitude may be an important influence on the amount of role strain experienced by the wife when both spouses work. Andrisani[10] examined this issue directly in an analysis of the job satisfaction of working women that utilized the National Longitudinal Survey of Mature Women, the data set employed in this study as well. This data set contains information on both the extent of the woman's child-care responsibilities and her perception of her husband's attitude toward her working outside the home. Andrisani found "that a husband's unfavorable attitude appears to be of greater consequence in terms of job dissatisfaction than the presence of a preschool child in the home or the need for child-care arrangements."[11] Thus there is evidence to support the contention that the competing demands of family and job result in lower-than-average levels of job satisfaction for mature women and, moreover, that the husband's unfavorable attitude toward her working is probably the major factor in reducing her job satisfaction.

The questions raised by this research on job satisfaction are provocative. The conclusions reached, however, are not entirely convincing because these studies—as so many other studies of married women in the labor force—make the implicit or explicit assumption that working wives in their thirties and forties have, typically, returned to paid employment after withdrawing to rear their children.[12] Yet, as we have seen, the NLS data confirm that there are two distinct patterns of employment over the life cycle for white, married women who choose both family and job. Some women wait until their children are of nursery school age or older before going back to work, while others leave the labor force only briefly or not at all when their children are born.

The question investigated in this chapter is whether women who select one or the other of these patterns may differ from each other in the satisfactions they derive from market work. Studies of job satisfaction that ignore this distinction and treat working wives as a homogeneous group may obscure important differences in the ways women react to their jobs and job opportunities, and in the ability of women to reconcile competing responsibilities at home and at work. Formally, this argument implies that models of job satisfaction among women that fail to distinguish between these two groups of women may be misspecified. This chapter re-examines the issue of job satisfaction among working wives, taking into account which of these life-cycle employment patterns has been followed. Special attention is paid to the effects of the woman's family responsibilities and her perception of her husband's attitude toward her employment on her level of job satisfaction.

Conceptual Framework

In analyzing women's job satisfaction, economists usually argue that the woman's age, health, family background, education, work experience, and the size of the labor force in the community in which she resides all proxy for the woman's ability to obtain a satisfying job.[13] Family circumstances—as measured by husband's attitude, presence of young children, husband's earnings, and own attitude toward the propriety of mothers working—are viewed as constraints. Wages and prestige status are the measurable rewards that the job provides.

However, the sex typing of occupations and the existence of segmented labor markets interact to confine most women to a fairly narrow range of jobs in the occupational structure. We would argue that this makes it unlikely that a straightforward relationship between education and work experience on the one hand and the quality of the job and job satisfaction on the other can be observed for women in either of our two groups. The relationship between labor market segmentation, these productivity proxies, and job satisfaction is likely to be complex and, in any event, would be difficult to analyze using the NLS data.[14] Our assumption is that both groups of women are confronted by essentially the same labor market structure and institutions, including discrimination. In view of the similarities in race, father's education, own education, and life-cycle patterns, this assumption seems tenable.

We will not, therefore, attempt to examine the argument that job satisfaction is related to age, health, family background, education, work experience, and size of the local labor force. These variables are included in our analysis simply as controls. This enables us to hold these variables constant while examining the effects of the variables with which we are concerned (such as husband's approval) on a woman's job satisfaction.

Employment Patterns and Job Satisfaction of Wives

The hypothesis examined in this chapter is that there are systematic differences between married women with children who leave the labor force for a protracted period and those who leave briefly or not at all that cause those factors related to the reconciliation of the competing demands of home and work responsibilities to differ in their effects on job satisfaction. Our argument is that the satisfaction a woman derives from her job may depend not only on the constraints imposed by her family situation and the rewards that the current job provides but is conditioned also by her goals and motives for working and by the wants and expectations that she attaches to her work activity.[15] The question, then, is whether a relationship can be found between the two observed patterns of employment over the life cycle and the expectations that a woman attaches to work activity that has testable implications for the woman's job satisfaction. This question is examined in the remainder of this section.

Orderly versus Chaotic Career Lines

In a thought-provoking article that never mentions women, but that Kahne and Hybels[16] were perceptive enough to include in their bibliography of recent papers related to women and work, Spilerman[17] characterizes the progression of jobs that a worker holds over his or her lifetime as either an orderly career line or a chaotic career line. To restate Spilerman's definitions, a chaotic career line is a collection of positions characterized by (1) "the absence of a linear progression—individuals tend to cycle among the positions," (2) "a similar average age of workers in each job—there is no age hierarchy because no job is a prerequisite for another on the list," and (3) "little difference in earnings or wages among the positions." This sort of career line, he points out, "can usefully be viewed as an array of activities requiring few special skills that might be obtained through prior employment in the career line, so each job serves, in practice, as an entry portal for new workers."[18] In contrast, an orderly career line is one in which the jobs which constitute the career line can be arranged so that "movement is predominantly in one direction"; (2) "older persons, on average, tend to be found in each succeeding position"; and (3) "each successive position in an orderly career brings an improvement in earnings and status."[19] Thus an orderly career line has the properties that are usually associated with informal notions of what is meant by a "career." Craft career lines and professional career lines—which correspond more closely to what are usually thought of as careers—are special sorts of orderly career lines, but not only the types possible.

These ideas warrant further elaboration. First, positions in a chaotic career line need not be unskilled. The jobs in a chaotic career line may require that the persons who fill them already have certain skills. However, these skills will not be upgraded through continuous employment in these positions. The positions held by typists, keypunch operators, and licensed practical nurses, for example, are not unskilled. But workers in these jobs essentially acquire their skills prior to employment. The skills are not later improved through investments by the firm in the further training of these employees, nor do these workers ordinarily progress to positions in which tasks are more complex. Of course, dead-end, unskilled jobs of all kinds belong to chaotic career lines. But even part-time, adjunct teaching positions at major universities may fall into this category.

A second point is that a particular job cannot be identified unambiguously with one or the other type of career line. While keypunch operator is not an entry-level position that leads ordinarily to subsequent positions in computer programming, a woman who plans to pursue an orderly career line may attend a trade school or take college courses in information science while supporting herself doing keypunching and acquire on her own the skills to progress to successive positions. Thus, while the position of keypunch operator is ordinarily a dead-end job that is found on a chaotic career line, it may nevertheless appear as an early position on the orderly career lines of some women.

Finally, prolonged absence from the labor force or intermittent attachment to it are both consistent with a chaotic career line, but not with an orderly one. Since each job in a chaotic career line functions as an entry-level position, while workers of all ages are found in all positions, and average wages do not vary much among the positions, a woman who finds herself on a chaotic career line has little to lose—in terms of her subsequent employment opportunities or her age-earnings profile—from leaving paid employment when her children are young. This is not true of an orderly career line. This type of career line ordinarily requires progression through a number of jobs and may be consistent with one or two short periods of absence from the labor force. Frequent or prolonged absences, however, are likely to jeopardize continued movement along the career line. Professional career lines, in particular, often involve a principal position in which the individual is employed continuously over a long period of time.

Thus one major source of systematic differences between the women in this study who left the labor force for a substantial period of time when they married or assumed responsibility for a child and those who did not may be differences in the kinds of career lines they desired to pursue or found themselves constrained by lack of alternatives to follow. This hypothesis cannot be tested directly using the NLS data set. However, aside from the intuitive appeal of this hypothesis, there is one striking difference between the two samples of women being compared here that supports this argument. If jobs are not to be viewed as independent entities, but are instead "linked components of coherent trajectories" so that subsequent changes in status and earnings are related to jobs held earlier in the career line, it may be instructive to compare the last job held by women in each of the two groups prior to the birth of their first child. For women who withdrew for three or more years, the median income for the occupation of the last job held prior to assuming responsibility for a child was, on average, only a little more than two thirds that of women who left for at most two years ($1,989 as compared with $2,860, in 1959 dollars). Prospects for subsequent earnings growth appear higher for women in the latter group, who would have correspondingly more to lose by becoming full-time homemakers.

Rewards from Work versus Family Responsibilities

Differences between the two groups of women that arise from differences in the kinds of career paths they follow have straightforward implications for the relative importance of the rewards from work vis-à-vis the constraints imposed by family responsibilities as factors influencing job satisfaction. The rewards from work, especially to the extent that they measure opportunities for future advancement, are likely to be of greater importance to those pursuing an orderly career. Competing demands from home may affect other measures of well-being (such as marital stability), but are not likely to affect job satisfaction. For women who are essentially cycling among positions in which wages and status do not vary much and continuous employment leads neither to higher skill levels nor greater rewards, conflicts between work and family responsibilities are likely to reduce job satisfaction.

Specifically, the hypothesis to be tested is that family demands, as measured by the presence of children and husband's attitude, will reduce the job satisfaction of those working wives who have returned to work after an absence of three or more years, but will not affect the job satisfaction of wives who withdrew for a shorter period following marriage or the birth of their first child. The job satisfaction of this latter group of women, it is hypothesized, will be most strongly related to the rewards from the jobs as measured by hourly earnings and prestige.

Empirical Analysis

Job satisfaction is measured by an ordinal level variable that has been assigned a value of 2 if the woman reported that she was highly satisfied with her 1972 job and a value of 1 otherwise. The dependent variable, quite clearly, is dichotomous, and the use of ordinary least squares regression analysis presents a number of difficulties which have been elaborated in the literature.[20] The model most appropriate in the case of a dichotomous, ordinal-level dependant variable is the probit model.[21] This model is similar to the familiar multivariate linear model, but it is designed for utilization in situations where the observed dependent variable is of this kind.

The figures in Table 4-1 indicate the relationship between job satisfaction and each explanatory variable. The variables are measured as follows: Late 30s is a dichotomous variable equal to 1 if the woman is 35–39 years of age and 0 otherwise; late 40s is a dichotomous variable equal to 1 if the woman is 45 to 49 years of age and 0 otherwise; the reference category is women 40 to 44 years of age; good health is a dichotomous variable equal to 1 if the woman's health did not limit her ability to work and 0 otherwise; father's education is a dichotomous variable equal to 1 if the woman's father completed 10 or more years of schooling and 0 otherwise; child less

Table 4-1 **The Effect of Selected Explanatory Variables on High Job Satisfaction in 1972 (standard errors in parentheses) [t-statistics in brackets]**

Variable	Mothers, Husbands Present Gap ≥ 3	Mothers, Husbands Present Gap < 3
Late 30s	0.0187 (0.2119) [0.385]	0.1952 (0.2461) [0.793]
Late 40s	0.0734 (0.1875) [0.392]	0.0281 (0.2642) [0.106]
Good health	0.2064 (0.2489) [0.829]	−0.1021 (0.3411) [−0.299]
Father's education	0.1177 (0.1873) [0.628]	−0.1929 (0.2430) [−0.794]
Years of schooling	−0.0091 (0.0474) [−0.192]	−0.0140 (0.0656) [−0.214]
Child < 6 years old[a]	−0.8765 (0.4709) [−1.861]*	0.5931 (0.4457) [1.331]
Child 6–17 years old[a]	−0.3122 (0.2696) [−1.158]	−0.2101 (0.3254) [−0.646]
Number of years worked 6 or more months by 1967	−0.0015 (0.0163) [−0.094]	0.0299 (0.0198) [1.509]
Number of weeks worked 1968–1972	−0.0018 (0.0017) [−1.059]	−0.0007 (0.0025) [−0.259]
Tenure on current job	0.0145 (0.0231) [0.627]	0.316 (0.0238) [1.326]
Job covered by union contract	−0.3437 (0.1886) [−1.823]*	0.0649 (0.2744) [0.237]
Full time (35 hours or more per week)	−0.0597 (0.1716) [−0.348]	−0.2484 (0.2654) [−0.936]

Table 4-1 (continued)

Variable	Mothers, Husbands Present Gap ≥ 3	Mothers, Husbands Present Gap < 3
Size of the local labor force	0.4255 (0.1651) [2.578]***	−0.1768 (0.2248) [−0.787]
Hourly earnings (in cents per hour)	0.0009 (0.0010) [0.969]	−0.0022 (0.0010) [−2.133]**
Social status of job	0.0100 (0.0078) [1.286]	0.0409 (0.0111) [3.683]***
Husband's annual earnings (in dollars)	0.0000 (0.0000) [0.334]	−0.0000 (0.0000) [−0.771]
Husband's attitude toward wife working[b]	0.5296 (0.1794) [2.952]***	0.1621 (0.2271) [0.714]
Own attitude toward mothers working[b]	0.0019 (0.1612) [0.012]	0.1738 (0.2173) [0.800]
Constant	−0.3525 (0.6655) [−0.530]	−0.8569 (0.8873) [−0.966]

Summary Statistics:		
Sample size, N	318	198
Percent correctly predicted	67.3%	63.1%
Likelihood ratio statistic	31.68**	29.05**
Degrees of freedom	18	18

Note: The dependent variable has been measured by an ordinal level variable assigned a value of 2 if the woman reported that she was highly satisfied, and a value of 1 otherwise.

[a] The omitted category (reference group) consists of respondents with no children 17 years of age or younger living at home.
[b] Measured by an ordinal level variable assigned a value of 1 in the case of a very favorable attitude, and a value of 0 otherwise.
*** Statistically significant at .01.
** Statistically significant at .05.
* Statistically significant at .10.

than 6 years old is a dichotomous variable that equals 1 if there is a child under the age of 6 in the household and 0 otherwise; child 6–17 years old is a dichotomous variable that equals 1 if the youngest child in household is between 6 and 17 years old and 0 otherwise; the reference category is no children 17 or younger in the household; job covered by union contract is a dichotomous variable equal to 1 if the job is so covered and 0 otherwise; full-time is a dichotomous variable equal to 1 if the woman works 35 hours or more per week and 0 otherwise; size of the local labor force is a dichotomous variable equal to 1 if the local labor force numbers 300,000 or less and 0 otherwise; husband's attitude is a dichotomous variable equal to 1 if he strongly approves and 0 otherwise; own attitude toward mothers working is a dichotomous variable equal to 1 if the index summarizing the woman's attitude has a score of 12–15 (highly favorable) and 0 otherwise. The remaining variables are continuous. Social status of the job is measured by the Bose index[22] which assumes values, for these groups of women, between 17 and 83. The units that apply to the other variables do not require clarification. Means for the explanatory variables are given in the appendix. Appendix tables A-4 and A-5 present the personal and work experience characteristics of the two groups of women.

The variables included provide measures of the women's social background, schooling, and post-schooling experience. For both groups of women we utilize data on father's education, educational attainment, age, health status, work experience, hours worked, tenure on the job, union coverage, and size of the local labor force. These variables are used for control purposes only, and their coefficients are reported but not discussed. The coefficient estimates can be interpreted, as in linear regression analysis, as the probability that a one unit change in the independent variable will result in the woman being highly satisfied with her job. A positive coefficient implies that the probability she will be highly satisfied with her job increases, a negative coefficient implies that it deceases.

Two summary statistics are reported. Percent correctly predicted is the percent of women for whom job satisfaction is correctly predicted by the set of explanatory variables included in the analysis. A second measure of goodness of fit which is more useful for statistical purposes, and more reliable given the maximum likelihood estimation procedure used to obtain the coefficients, is the likelihood ratio statistic. In large samples this statistic is distributed approximately chi-square with a number of degrees of freedom equal to the number of parameters.

The model estimated here predicts the level of job satisfaction correctly for 67.3 percent of the women in the first group, and for 63.1 percent of those in the second. Moreover, the likelihood ratio statistic is significant in both cases at the .05 level.

The results presented in Table 4-1 clearly support our hypothesis. For a woman who was out of the labor force for a period of three or more years, husband's approval of her working increases the probability that she will be highly satisfied with her job. This coefficient is statistically significant at the .01 level. For women who left the work force for less than three years, however, husband's approval does not significantly affect the level of job satisfaction. Again, the presence of a preschool child in the household significantly reduces the level of job satisfaction of women who withdrew for three or more years. Presence of a young child reduces the probability that a woman in this group will be highly satisfied. Child care responsibilities, however, do not reduce job satisfaction of women in the second group.

On the other hand, neither hourly earnings nor the social status of the job is associated with higher levels of job satisfaction for those women who re-entered the labor force after an absence of three or more years. By contrast, these are the only explanatory variables included in our analysis that significantly affect the job satisfaction of women whose absence from paid employment was under three years. For this latter group of women, an increase in the social status of the job is associated with an increase in the probability that the woman is highly satisfied with her job.

The finding that higher hourly earnings are associated with lower levels of satisfaction which emerges from our analysis has also been reported in other studies of the job satisfaction of mature women, where it has been viewed as inexplicable.[23] We might speculate that job satisfaction for women pursuing an orderly career line is more closely related to the prospects for further advancement associated with the current position than to the immediate rewards the position provides. Holding education, hours, and work experience constant, women with lower earnings may be in positions in which on-the-job training investments by the firm and subsequent opportunities to progress to more rewarding positions are greater. Those with higher earnings may feel they have gone as far as they can, and this may contribute to a reduction in the probability that they will be highly satisfied.

Summary

This chapter has demonstrated that the pattern of employment over the life cycle has major implications for women's job satisfaction. It is, indeed, important in analyzing the job satisfaction of working wives to distinguish between women who withdraw from the labor force at the time of marriage or the birth of the first child and do not return for three or more years and those who withdraw for a shorter period of time. Ignoring this distinction and treating working wives as a homogeneous group yields misleading results. Conclusions may be drawn and applied to both groups of women that are, in fact, accurate for only one of the groups. We have argued that there are systematic differences in the ways that these two groups of women react to their jobs, and in their ability to reconcile the competing demands of home and work on their time and energy. This chapter has shown that, in fact, such differences do exist. As hypothesized, the job satisfaction of women in the first group proved to be significantly affected by family responsibilities as measured by the presence of young children and husband's attitude. The job satisfaction of women in the second group, on the contrary, was found to be related to the rewards from work and not to pressures from home. We argued that these systematic differences arise because of differences in the sorts of career lines being followed by the women in these groups. We suggested that women who withdraw for a protracted period are pursuing chaotic career lines, while those whose absence is short are trying to pursue orderly career lines. Our findings lend credence to this argument, but we were not able to test it directly.

Endnotes

1. Eileen Appelbaum and Ross Koppel, "Is Part-Time Work a Successful Resolution to the Role Conflicts of Working Mothers?" Paper presented at the meetings of the International Sociological Association, IX World Congress of Sociology, Uppsala, Sweden, August 1978; R. Rapoport and R. Rapoport, *Dual Career Families Reexamined: New Integration of Work and Family* (New York: Harper, 1976); A. Parelius, "Emerging Sex-Role Attitudes, Expectations and Strains among College Women," *Journal of Marriage and the Family*, 37 (February 1975), pp. 146–153; L. W. Hoffman and F. I. Nye, eds., *Working Mothers* (San Francisco: Jossey-Bass, 1974); L. L. Holmstrom, *The Two Career Family* (Cambridge, Mass.: Schenkman, 1973).
2. Julia A. Ericksen, "An Analysis of the Journey to Work for Women," *Social Problems*, 24 (April 1977), pp. 428–435; J. C. Darian, "Convenience of Work

and the Job Constraint of Children," *Demography, 12* (May 1975), pp. 245–255;
L. Bailyn, "Family Constraints on Women's Work" in R. B. Kundsin, ed.,
Women and Success (New York: William Morrow, 1973); Glen G. Cain, *Married Women in the Labor Force: An Economic Analysis* (Chicago: University of
Chicago Press, 1966).

3. D. T. Hall and F. E. Gordon, "Career Choices of Married Women," *Journal of
Applied Psychology, 58* (January 1973), pp. 42–48.

4. Joseph H. Pleck, Graham L. Staines, and Linda Lang, "Conflicts Between
Work and Family Life," *Monthly Labor Review, 103* (March 1980), pp. 29–31.

5. See Sandra L. Hofferth and Kristin A. Moore, "Women's Employment and
Marriage" in Ralph E. Smith, ed., *The Subtle Revolution: Women at Work*
(Washington, D.C.: The Urban Institute, 1979), especially the literature reviewed on pp. 116–122.

6. *Ibid.*, p. 119.

7. R. P. Quinn, G. L. Staines, and M. R. McCullough, *Job Satisfaction: Is There a
Trend?*, U.S. Department of Labor, Manpower Research Monograph No. 3
(1974).

8. *Ibid.*, p. 11.

9. J. H. Pleck, "The Work-Family Role System," *Social Problems, 24* (April 1977),
pp. 417–427; R. J. Burke and T. Weir, "Relationship of Wives' Employment to
Husband, Wife and Pair Satisfaction and Performance," *Journal of Marriage
and the Family, 38* (May 1976), pp. 179–187; M. M. Poloma and T. N. Garland,
"The Myth of the Egalitarian Family: Familial Roles and the Professionally
Employed Wife" in A. Theodore, ed., *The Professional Woman* (Cambridge,
Mass.: Schenkman, 1971); and L. Bailyn, "Career and Family Orientations of
Husbands and Wives in Relation to Marital Happiness," *Human Relations, 23*
(April 1970), pp. 97–113.

10. Paul J. Andrisani, "Job Satisfaction among Working Women," *Signs: Journal of
Women in Culture and Society, 3* (Spring 1978) pp. 588–607.

11. *Ibid.*, p. 604.

12. Andrisani, *op. cit.*, is quite explicit. He writes, on p. 588, "The extent of job
satisfaction among women is an important aspect of their labor market experience, for it may signify the degree to which they have made a successful
accommodation to the world of work. The issue is especially important in the
case of women in their thirties and forties, because the children of those in this
age group are generally of school age, and decreasing home responsibilities
allow considerable reentry into the work force."

13. B. Carroll, *Job Satisfaction: A Review of the Literature,* Key Issues Series, No. 3
(Ithaca, N.Y.: New York State School of Industrial and Labor Relations, 1973);
Andrisani, *op. cit.*

14. Clifford B. Hawley and William T. Bielby, "Research Uses of the National
Longitudinal Survey of Data on Mature Women" in *Women's Changing Role at
Home and on the Job,* National Commision for Manpower Policy, Special Report No. 26 (Washington, D.C.: U.S. Government Printing Office, September
1978).

15. Some of these issues are raised in K. J. Russell, "Variations in Orientation to
Work and Job Satisfaction," *Sociology of Work and Occupations, 2* (November
1975), pp. 299–322.

16. Hilda Kahne and Judith Hybels, *Work and Family Issues: A Bibliography of Economic and Related Social Science Research*, Working Paper No. 33 (Wellesley, Mass.: Wellesley Center for Research on Women, 1978).
17. Seymour Spilerman, "Careers, Labor Market Structure, and Socioeconomic Achievement," *American Journal of Sociology, 83* (November 1977), pp. 551–593.
18. *Ibid.*, p. 578.
19. *Ibid.*
20. H. Theil, *Economics and Information Theory* (Amsterdam: North-Holland Publishing Company, 1967); and H. Theil, "On the Estimation of Relationships Involving Qualitative Variables," *American Journal of Sociology, 76* (July 1970), pp. 103–154.
21. R. D. McKelvey and W. Zaroina, "A Statistical Model for the Analysis of Ordinal Dependent Variables," *Journal of Mathematical Sociology, 4* (1975), pp. 103–120.
22. C. Bose, "Women and Jobs: Sexual Influences on Occupational Prestige," Ph.D. dissertation, The Johns Hopkins University, 1973.
23. P. J. Andrisani, "Levels and Trends in Job Satisfaction, 1966–1972," in P. J. Andrisani with E. Appelbaum, R. Koppel, and R. Miljus, *Work Attitudes and Labor Market Experience* (New York: Praeger Special Studies, 1978).

Chapter 5

EMPIRICAL ANALYSIS OF MATURE WOMEN'S SUCCESSFUL RE-ENTRY

Women who re-enter the labor force after having dropped out entirely for a period of time experience varying degrees of success in making this transition. For many, the change is not easy. The recent drafting of legislation to aid displaced homemakers and the passage in 1978 of a bill designed to create more part-time civil service jobs at every grade level have highlighted the difficulties faced by women returning to work. Two different kinds of concerns confront women who are returning to work. The first set of problems is related to the lack of an underlying social-support system for women who combine the roles of wife, mother, and worker. Despite the large increase in the last 35 years in the number of working wives and mothers, socioeconomic structures have been exceedingly slow in accommodating the changes in family needs that have accompanied the influx of young married women into the labor force. The provision of child care remains woefully inadequate, and the design and location of facilities that would promote the parent-child relationship without requiring mothers to jeopardize career goals, though prevalent in some parts of Europe, are not even under discussion in the United States. Flexibility in work hours to allow parents to spend part of the regular workday with their children when necessary and to catch up on work on the job during mornings, evenings, and weekends, as well as an increase in the number of substantive part-time jobs, would also enable mothers to meet day-to-day responsibilities without sacrificing career development. While some progress in this area has been made, flexitime arrangements are not generally available, and most part-time jobs, as the next chapter demonstrates, pay low wages that do not fairly compensate a woman for the skills she brings to the job and do not provide her with opportunities to progress on the job. Changes here will have to be accomplished through the political process and cannot be achieved through the discretionary actions of individual women.

The second set of concerns, in contrast, is related to the ways in which individual women have prepared for their return to the labor force. Most visible has been the increase in the numbers of mature white women pursuing a college degree. The number of students age 35 and over rose by 100,000 between October 1974 and October 1976, for example, with almost all of the increase occurring among white women enrolled in degree programs at the college undergraduate level.[1] However, preparation by women for a return to work encompasses a wide range of activities, some of them undertaken prior to withdrawing from paid employment to attend to children and household responsibilities and others pursued during the years out of the labor force. Women engage in these activities in the hope that they will smooth re-entry into the work force and will result in higher wages, higher status jobs, and greater satisfaction with work. The actions women take in preparing for a return to work are not entirely discretionary—economic and social constraints limit the available choices, often severely. Still, getting a high school diploma, enrolling in degree programs, taking college courses for enrichment, and acquiring vocational skills are all things that women do in order to help themselves. The important question for these women is: What works? Do any or all of these activities make a difference when women return to paid employment? And what of the actions taken by women in the early stages of their lives? Do any of these matter by the time they are ready to return to work?

This chapter addresses these concerns, presenting an empirical analysis of the effects of these actions and examining whether any of these factors contribute to the successful re-entry of mature women into the work force. The effects on hourly earnings, prestige, and job satisfaction of a host of non-household, non-market activities in which these women have engaged are examined. The activities include preparation for a career (years of schooling, high school curriculum, college major, shorthand and typing) and post-school investments in human capital. In addition, the effects on successful re-entry of the attributes of jobs held early in the career, prior to withdrawing from the labor force, are also explored.

Theoretical Perspectives

There are two competing views of how workers achieve success in the labor market. In the human capital approach, the individual is the unit of analysis and emphasis is on investments in human capital made by the individual's parental family, those investments that the individual chooses to obtain through formal schooling, and post-school investments that the individual chooses to carry out in extracurricular or on-the-job training programs. These personal sorts of investment are viewed as explanations of differences in productivity among workers, and hence as explanations of differences in labor market outcomes with respect to wages and occupational status.[2]

In the dual (or, more generally, the stratified) labor market approach, it is the structure of labor markets and the unequal access of workers to entry into particular job clusters that is largely responsible for labor market outcomes. Access to higher-paying, upper-strata jobs is based partly on superficial characteristics such as sex and ethnicity, with women and blacks largely denied entrance. Educational requirements for jobs, in this view, are not directly related to job content and worker productivity, but provide employers with an additional inexpensive screening device for filtering workers into particular job clusters. In addition to paying generally higher wages, upper-strata jobs provide opportunities for training and career advancement and hence make possible later growth in earnings and advances in occupational status. Lower-strata jobs neither utilize fully the individual's prior educational achievements nor provide opportunities for the development of additional work competencies. Since employment in upper-strata jobs is an essential component of the skill acquisition process, denying women, blacks, and other minorities entrance to these job clusters consigns them to the lower end of both the skill and earnings distributions.[3]

Limitations of Survey Data

It is generally difficult to sort out the differences in these approaches using survey data on the socioeconomic attributes of individuals. The finding that higher wages are associated with more schooling can be interpreted either as evidence that better-educated workers are more productive or that more credentials are required for en-

trance into better-paying, upper-strata jobs. Similarly, both approaches recognize the importance of skills acquired on the job for
career advancement and earnings growth, and thus both approaches
suggest that the characteristics of jobs held by an individual at an
earlier career stage will have a major impact on subsequent labor
market experiences. In a recent summary of the research uses of the
NLS data for the cohort of mature women, Hawley and Bielby point
up the difficulty of using these data to analyze the demand side of
the labor market:[4]

> [D]ual and segmented labor market theories have offered explanations
> of socioeconomic inequality that focus on institutional barriers to neo-
> classical market mechanisms. . . . These approaches often stress the
> importance of attributes of jobs and their hierarchical arrangement in
> occupational structure.
>
> Applied to the different labor market outcome of men and women,
> the "demand" or "structural" theories suggest that employer behavior
> and the distribution of job opportunities condition family decision
> making and the occupational choices of women. . . . Direct tests of
> many aspects of these theories require data not attainable from repre-
> sentative social surveys of individuals: for example, attributes of in-
> dustries, the social and technical organization of work, and the actions
> of employers.

One serious difficulty in utilizing the NLS data base, therefore, is
that it constrains the researcher to focus on "supply-side" considerations to the almost total exclusion of factors on the "demand-side." In
particular, Thurow's[5] suggestion that queuing processes place women
at a disadvantage relative to men and arguments advanced by Gordon[6] and Bowles and Gintis[7] relating class domination and exploita-
tion to the position of most women in the labor market can neither
be introduced directly in the formulation of research questions nor
confirmed unambiguously by research results based on these data.
We acknowledge this limitation at the outset. Moreover, we recognize that caution must be used in interpreting results obtained using
the NLS since the measured outcomes (wages, prestige) are the
resultant of both labor supply and labor demand effects, while the
NLS provides data directly only for the labor supply aspects.

There is, then, a severe restriction on the use of these data to
resolve major theoretical issues related to the wage and status attainment process for mature women returning to paid employment.
Consequently, we have chosen to address in this chapter the more
limited question of whether, *given* the existing structure of the labor
market and of available opportunities, any of the things done by
white women who are following a traditional life-cycle labor force

pattern are effective in improving their chances of success when they re-enter the labor force. This is an empirical question of no small consequence for which the NLS, given its longitudinal character, is uniquely appropriate. In particular, the extent to which preparations for a career and characteristics of early labor market experience affect re-entrance is an issue with important policy implications for young women. Jusenius and Sandell[8] suggest that young women tend to underestimate the likelihood that they will re-enter the labor force after their children are enrolled in school. At the same time, several studies[9] report findings that are consistent with the view that young women who do not plan to work in later years acquire less general training in job skills in the early stages of their working lives. Combining these two arguments, Shapiro and Carr[10] suggest that "it seems likely that many young women will be at a serious disadvantage if they re-enter the labor force after raising a family." They argue that appropriate policies directed to young women should include (1) appraising young women of the likelihood that they will be in the labor force after their children enter school, (2) encouraging them to prepare adequately for this experience, and (3) utilizing counseling and vocational guidance in both secondary schools and colleges for this purpose.

Alternatively, it can be argued that although the evidence suggests that expected future labor force attachment is an important determinant of the on-the-job training acquired by young women in the initial stages of their careers, it may nevertheless be the case that women with such training are *not* more successful in re-entering the labor force. Instead, acquired skills may become obsolete or deteriorate rapidly during periods of disuse, or women with family responsibilities may seek less demanding jobs when re-entering employment and may not make use of the skills acquired earlier, or employers may discriminate against mature women or women with a history of having withdrawn from the labor force, so that such women will not be hired for jobs requiring the previously learned skills. If this view proves to be correct, young women anticipating a discontinuous work experience might be better advised to forego the training opportunities and the associated lower initial wages of jobs that offer on-the-job training, and opt instead for the job paying highest initial wages. Given the realities facing mature women seeking re-employment, the possibility exists that the current behavior of young women might, in fact, be economically rational. Women certainly have a direct interest in knowing which is the correct view.

A related issue is the extent to which such activities as participating in a training program, attending adult education courses, or enrolling in college on a part-time basis affect re-entry. To a greater or lesser extent, all of these activities represent further investments in human capital and may be expected to increase both the skills and the credentials of the women engaged in them. Whether these skills and/or credentials can be translated into higher-status jobs, better wages, and increased job satisfaction, however, is a question that can best be answered empirically.

Factors Contributing to Success in 1972

Three measures of successful re-entry of mature women into the labor force are examined in this section. They are 1972 wages, measured in cents per hour; prestige status of the 1972 job, measured by the Bose index;[11] and extent of satisfaction with the 1972 job, operationalized as a dichotomous variable that assumes the value 1 if the woman is highly satisfied with her job and the value 0 otherwise. Ordinary least squares regression techniques are utilized in the analysis of wages and prestige status. The wage equation was also specified using the log of wages as the dependent variable. The substantive results are the same as when wages are used. We therefore report the results using wages as the dependent variable because of the greater simplicity this allows in interpreting the findings. As explained in the previous chapter, ordinary least squares is not an appropriate technique for analyzing an ordinal-level dependent variable; hence we have employed a linear probability (probit) model in analyzing job satisfaction.[12]

Effects of Demographic and Work
Experience Variables

Table 5-1 presents the effects on wages, prestige, and high job satisfaction of the demographic and work experience variables that previous research by sociologists and economists suggests may have important effects. These variables include age, health status, years of schooling, father's education, marital and family status, region of residence, size of the local labor force, general work experience, tenure on current job, usual hours worked, and union coverage of current job. The effects of these variables on wages, prestige, and

Table 5-1 **Effect of Demographic Characteristics and Work Experience on Wages, Prestige, and Job Satisfaction in 1972 for White Women, Gap ≥ 3 (t-statistics in parentheses)**

Variable	Wages	Prestige	High Job Satisfaction
Late 30s, 1972	4.945	1.021	0.086
	(0.386)	(0.707)	(0.411)
Late 40s, 1972	4.419	−2.637	0.245
	(0.403)	(−2.129)**	(1.313)
Good health, 1972	15.231	1.708	0.353
	(1.047)	(1.041)	(1.445)
Years of schooling	14.828	3.640	0.068
	(6.261)***	(3.115)***	(1.710)*
Father has 10 or more	32.390	2.438	−0.055
years of schooling	(3.024)***	(2.017)**	(−0.309)
Husband present, 1972	7.963	2.549	0.245
	(0.646)	(1.833)*	(1.182)
Child under 6 years of	28.255	−3.147	−0.774
age, 1972	(1.354)	(−1.337)	(−2.226)**
Child 6–17 years of age,	0.449	−0.855	0.040
1972	(0.031)	(−0.527)	(0.176)
Years worked 6 months or	1.945	0.241	−0.005
more through 1967	(2.005)**	(2.203)**	(−0.303)
Weeks worked 1968–1972	0.242	0.023	−0.002
	(2.372)**	(2.028)**	(−1.342)
Works full time (35 hours	15.737	0.481	−0.027
or more), 1972	(1.509)	(0.409)	(−0.161)
Tenure on current job,	3.120	0.077	0.011
1972	(2.312)**	(0.507)	(0.509)
Job covered by union	46.598	−1.370	−0.453
contract, 1972	(4.061)***	(−1.058)	(−2.509)**
Resides in South, 1972	−14.168	0.779	−0.016
	(−1.248)	(0.608)	(−0.083)
Local labor force numbers	−34.013	−1.322	0.270
less than 300,000	(−3.450)***	(−1.186)	(1.682)*
Constant	0.059	−0.558	−0.880
	(0.002)	(−0.134)	(−1.398)
Mean Value	274 cents	46.98	.416
N	378	377	320
R²	0.314	0.433	
F	11.029***	18.364***	
Percent correctly predicted			61.9%
Likelihood ratio statistic			25.134**

*** Statistically significant at p < .01.
** Statistically significant at p < .05.
* Statistically significant at p < .10.

job satisfaction will be considered only briefly since we are concerned mainly with the impact of other sets of variables. However, these demographic and work experience variables do provide the context within which the effects of those other sets of determinants are examined. They are included as control variables in the regressions reported in Tables 5-2 through 5-5, in which we consider the effects of steps taken to prepare for a career while still in school, the effects of post-school investments in human capital, and the effects of selected characteristics of jobs held earlier in the career on wages, prestige, and job satisfaction following re-entry.

Beginning with the demographic characteristics, we note the counter-intuitive finding that being in good health does not appear to affect wages, prestige, or job satisfaction. Age affects neither wages nor job satisfaction, but women in their late 40s have less prestigious jobs than younger women. This is probably attributable to the more limited range of jobs available to women at the time these women re-entered the work force. Age discrimination is another possible explanation, but the fact that these women do not earn less than women in their late 30s or early 40s suggests that this may not be an important factor. The positive effects of education on earnings and prestige status, which have been widely noted in the literature, are confirmed for our sample. These effects have been attributed variously to the use of credentials as a cheap screening device by employers,[13] or to the role of education in increasing labor productivity.[14]

Sociologists have also argued that socioeconomic background is an important determinant of both earnings and occupational achievement.[15] Socioeconomic background is measured in this study by father's education and exhibits the strong, positive effects on earnings and prestige predicted in the status attainment literature. Somewhat surprisingly, perhaps, the presence of children, even young children, at home does not depress either wages or prestige status of the jobs held by the women in our sample. The presence of young children at home does, however, reduce the job satisfaction of these women, a finding which we discussed at length in Chapter 4. Women in small labor markets earn substantially less than those in large. Prestige status of the jobs held by women in small labor markets also tends to be lower, but this relationship does not quite reach statistical significance. On the other hand, women in small labor markets are more likely to be highly satisfied with their jobs. This may be due to their holding jobs located closer to their homes.

To the extent that this reduces tensions associated with working, it may contribute to the job satisfaction of this group of women (see Chapter 4). Region of residence affects neither job satisfaction nor prestige, but living in the South, where the cost of living is somewhat lower, does have a negative though not quite statistically significant effect on wages.

Turning to the work experience variables, we observe that the amount of work experience, including both the number of years through 1967 in which six or more months were worked and the number of weeks worked between 1968 and 1972, has a significant effect on wages and prestige. Women who work full time tend to earn more, but do not hold higher-status jobs. Similarly, the wages of these women increase with length of time with the current employer, but not the prestige status of the job held. The finding that none of the work experience variables affects job satisfaction for these women is consistent with our findings in Chapter 4, where we argued that it is primarily the extent to which home and job responsibilities conflict that influences the job satisfaction of this group of women. Finally, holding a job covered by a union contract has a large positive effect on the wages of women in this sample. Despite the substantial improvement in hourly earnings associated with union coverage, those women in covered employment were much less likely to be satisfied with their jobs.

Effects of Steps Taken While Still in School

We turn next to the variables of primary interest to us. In Table 5-2 we consider the effects of steps taken while still in school in order to prepare for possible employment on our measures of successful re-entry. Four aspects of career preparation are considered: choice of high school curriculum, achievement in high school English, taking typing or shorthand in high school, and choice of college major. Our results indicate that while the number of years of schooling completed by 1967 is an important determinant of wages and prestige, how these years are spent has very little effect. Among high school graduates who did not go on to college by 1967, the choice of a vocational or commercial curriculum instead of an academic curriculum affects neither wages nor prestige status of the 1972 job. Similarly, taking high school typing and/or shorthand does not affect wages or prestige of jobs held after re-entry. This result holds even though years of schooling is controlled for, so that even within

Table 5-2   Net Effect of Steps Taken While in School to Prepare for a Career on
Wages, Prestige, and Job Satisfaction in 1972 for White Women, Gap
$\geq 3^a$ (t-statistics in parentheses)

Aspect of Career Preparation	Wages	Prestige	High Job Satisfaction
High School Curriculum (reference category: academic curriculum, no college)			
Not a high school graduate	−33.114	−10.413	−0.650
	(−2.309)**	(−6.418)***	(−1.552)
Vocational or commercial curriculum	6.620	1.574	−0.232
	(0.593)	(1.244)	(−1.308)*
Some college or more	103.445	20.922	0.331
	(5.736)***	(10.255)***	(0.662)
Self Perception of English Achievement in High School (reference category: medium achievement in English)			
High achievement	29.305	1.724	0.318
	(1.575)*	(1.124)	(1.331)*
Low achievement	−8.445	−1.492	−0.101
	(−0.552)	(−1.275)	(−0.596)
High School Typing or Shorthand	−8.055	0.554	−0.009
	(−0.760)	(0.458)	(−0.048)
College Major (reference category: education or other profession)			
1–14 years of schooling	−99.903	−17.960	−0.270
	(−4.861)***	(−7.154)***	(−0.645)
Mathematics, science, liberal arts	30.354	9.218	−0.560
	(0.831)	(2.066)**	(−0.941)

[a] In all cases multiple regression techniques have been used to control for individual differences in age, health status, education, father's education, marital and family status, region of residence, size of local labor force, years of work experience through 1967, weeks of work experience 1968–1972, hours worked, tenure on current job, union coverage.

*** $p < .01$, ** $p < .05$, * $p < .10$

categories of educational attainment this kind of training does not seem to matter. High achievement in high school English tends to increase wages, and low achievement has a slight, depressing effect on prestige status, but both of these are weak relationships. Choice of college major, on the other hand, has a large and significant impact on prestige status of the 1972 job. Majoring in mathematics, science, or liberal arts increases the prestige score of the 1972 job by nine points as compared with majoring in education or other fields. The effect of choice of college major on wages is not significant. Choice of college major does not affect job satisfaction, though there is a weak relationship between job satisfaction and high school curriculum or achievement in high school English. Women who select the vocational or commercial curriculum are less likely to be highly satisfied with their jobs, while those doing well in high school English are more likely to enjoy their jobs.

Effects of Post-School Preparation on Job Success

In contrast to the weak effects that choices of courses and programs made while in school appear to have, post-school investments in human captial made by these women have major consequences for wages and prestige in 1972, increasing both significantly (see Table 5-3). Completing a training program by 1972 increases wages on average by 15 cents an hour and improves the prestige status of the job by 3.5 points. Women completing professional, technical, or managerial programs benefit most, earning 32 cents an hour more than women without such training and holding jobs that are 8.3 points higher on the Bose prestige scale. These effects of training, it should be remembered, are net of the effects of years of schooling. The length of the training program is also significant, with longer training programs leading to both higher wages and higher-status jobs. Obtaining a professional certificate is perhaps most beneficial of all, increasing wages by nearly a dollar an hour and prestige score by 10 points. Obtaining a trade certificate does not have a significant effect on wages and prestige in our analysis. However, Kiefer[16] has demonstrated that cross-section bias may be substantial when post-training wage rates are regressed on background variables and a dummy variable such as the one used here to indicate whether a certificate has been obtained. That is, the position of the women who obtained a trade certificate might have been much worse prior to obtaining the trade certificate, but our analysis does not measure the improvement. Returning to school for additional courses is another effective step that women can take to improve their position in the labor market after re-entry. Controlling for the effects of educational achievement in 1967, we find that taking courses toward a high school diploma increases the prestige status of the 1972 job by 5 points, taking courses toward a college degree increases it by nearly 9 points and just taking other courses increases it by 4 points. Taking

Table 5-3 Net Effects of Post-School Investments in Human Capital on Wages, Prestige, and Job Satisfaction in 1972 for White Women, Gap ⩾ 3[a] (t-statistics in parentheses)

Aspect of Post-School Investment	Wages	Prestige	High Job Satisfaction
Training Program Completed by 1972	15.497	3.463	0.104
	(1.813)**	(3.381)***	(0.679)
Type of Training Completed by 1972 (reference category: no training program completed)			
Professional, technical, managerial	31.703	8.297	1.064
	(1.858)**	(4.111)***	(2.230)**
Clerical	5.534	2.207	−0.020
	(0.514)	(1.728)**	(−0.106)
Other	8.100	2.471	−0.003
	(0.786)	(2.026)**	(−0.018)
Length of Training Program Completed			
Months of training through	1.968	0.076	0.031
1967	(3.153)***	(1.008)	(2.192)**
Weeks of training 1968–1972	0.618	0.087	0.004
	(3.141)***	(3.689)***	(0.850)
Certificate Obtained by 1972	49.984	6.885	0.255
	(4.288)***	(5.037)***	(1.117)
Type of Certificate Obtained (reference category: no certificate)			
Trade certificate	−3.677	0.208	0.140
	(−0.148)	(0.070)	(0.246)
Professional certificate	96.787	9.944	−0.006
	(5.739)***	(4.937)***	(−0.017)
Additional Education Courses (reference category: no additional schooling)			
Courses for a high school diploma	−16.528	5.087	−0.093
	(−0.741)	(1.907)**	(−0.362)
Courses for a college degree	126.666	8.739	4.792
	(3.909)***	.(2.256)**	(0.077)
Other schooling	33.969	3.915	−0.038
	(2.324)**	(2.240)**	(−0.072)

[a] In all cases multiple regression techniques have been used to control for individual differences in age, health status, education, father's education, marital and family status, region of residence, size of local labor force, years of work experience through 1967, weeks of work experience 1968–1972, hours worked, tenure on current job, union coverage.

*** $p < .01$, ** $p < .05$, * $p < .10$

courses for a college degree has the striking effect of increasing hourly earnings by $1.27 an hour. Taking courses toward a high school degree does not significantly affect wages (here, again, cross-section bias may prevent our measuring improvements from a more negative to a less negative position) while just taking courses increases wages by 34 cents an hour.

Post-school investments in human capital do not exhibit the same systematic effects in increasing the probability of high job satisfaction that they exhibit in improving wages and prestige status. Completing a professional, technical, or managerial program does increase the likelihood that a woman will be highly satisfied with her job. The number of months of training completed by 1967 also has a significant effect on job satisfaction. None of the other aspects of post-school investment considered here, however, have any effect at all.

Effects of Early Jobs on Later Career Success

Of great importance is the finding that the characteristics of jobs held earlier in a woman's career, prior to her leaving the labor force to attend to household tasks and to rear her children, affect both wages and the prestige of jobs held after re-entry. The quality and even the availability of on-the-job training varies widely across jobs. Proponents of the theory that labor markets are segmented argue that getting into the right job cluster early in the career is perhaps the major determinant of subsequent labor market experiences,[17] though little had previously been known about whether this holds as well for women with a discontinuous work history that includes an extended period of absence. Three characteristics are used to measure the quality of jobs held early in the career: median education of incumbents in that job in 1960, median income earned by incumbents in that job in 1959, and prestige status of the job. Two jobs (for some women they may be the same job) are examined. They are the job held longest between school and marriage, and the job held longest in the period prior to withdrawal from the paid labor force. Our analysis indicates (see Table 5-4) that getting a "good" job in these early periods is crucial in affecting labor market position after re-entry. Median education and prestige status of these early jobs affects both wages and prestige status of the 1972 job, with better jobs in the early stages leading to better jobs subsequently. The

Table 5-4 Net Effects of Selected Characteristics of Longest Job Held between School and Marriage (Job 1) and Longest Job Held prior to Withdrawal from the Labor Force (Job L) on Wages, Prestige, and Job Satisfaction in 1972 for White Women, Gap ≥ 3[a] (t-statistics in parentheses)

Aspect of Job 1, Job L	Wages	Prestige	High Job Satisfaction
Median Education in Job in 1960			
Job 1	0.756	0.237	—
	(2.151)**	(6.256)***	
Job L	0.819	0.270	0.011
Median Income in Job in 1959	(2.242)**	(6.919)***	(1.683)**
Job 1	0.000	0.002	—
	(0.059)	(2.441)**	
Job L	0.006	0.000	0.000
	(2.203)**	(0.869)	(1.356)*
Prestige Status of Job			
Job 1	0.903	0.316	—
	(1.803)*	(5.826)***	
Job L	1.140	0.366	0.012
	(2.217)**	(6.645)***	(1.393)*
Occupation of Last Job Held Prior to Dropping Out of Labor Force (reference category: clerical or sales)			
Professional, technical, or managerial occupation	57.180	6.786	0.042
	(3.826)***	(3.955)***	(0.139)
Other occupation	−15.154	−5.159	−0.428
	(−1.502)	(−4.453)***	(−2.379)**

[a] In all cases multiple regression techniques have been used to control for individual differences in age, health status, education, father's education, marital and family status, region of residence, size of local labor force, years of work experience through 1967, weeks of work experience 1968–1972, hours worked, tenure on current job, union coverage.

*** $p < .01$, ** $p < .05$, * $p < .10$

effects of median income are not as uniform, with last job held affecting 1972 wages but not prestige status and job held between school and marriage affecting prestige status of the 1972 job but not wages. Job satisfaction in 1972 is also affected by the quality of the last job held prior to leaving the labor force. Women who had previously held jobs in which the median education was higher, or in

Table 5-5   Net Effects of Years Worked Six or More Months between (1) School
             and Marriage and (2) Marriage and Child on Wages, Prestige and Job
             Satisfaction in 1972 for White Women, Gap ≥ 3[a] (t-statistics in pa-
             rentheses)

	Wages	Prestige	High Job Satisfaction
(1) Years worked 6 or more months between school and marriage	0.729 (0.471)	0.545 (3.043)***	−0.018 (−0.598)
(2) Years worked 6 or more months between marriage and child	4.541 (2.287)**	0.492 (2.147)**	0.077 (2.076)**

[a] In analyzing the effects of these two variables, multiple regression techniques have been used to control for individual differences in age, health status, education, father's education, marital and family status, region of residence, size of local labor force, weeks of work experience 1968–1972, hours worked, tenure on current job, union coverage.

*** $p < .01$, ** $p < .05$, * $p < .10$

which the median income was higher, or which were more prestigious were more likely to be highly satisfied with their 1972 job than other women. Perhaps holding a good job early in the career leads to more favorable attitudes toward work. The effect on job satisfaction, however, is much weaker than on wages or prestige.

Another aspect of the last job held prior to dropping out of the work force—occupation of the job—is also examined. We find that women who held professional, technical, or managerial jobs early in their careers earned more and held more prestigious jobs in 1972 than those who had done sales or clerical work, while those who had jobs other than these (craft, operatives, service) early on fared even more poorly after returning to work. Having held one of these "other" jobs at an earlier stage also reduced the probability of being highly satisfied with the 1972 job.

Finally, in Table 5-5, we examine the effect of years of work experience in each of two periods on labor market position in 1972. We find that the number of years in which a woman worked six or more months between marriage and first child increases wages, prestige, and job satisfaction; while only prestige is affected by the number of years between school and marriage in which she worked six or more months.

Factors Contributing to Advances Between 1972 and 1976

As we saw in the previous section, years of schooling, post-school investments in human capital, and attributes of jobs held early in the career all have important effects on the labor market attainments of women who have returned to work. The question we would like to examine next is whether advances made over the 1972–1976 period were systematically affected by these variables as well. As the job satisfaction questions were not asked again in 1976 and the Bose index of the 1976 job is not available in the public use tapes, we are limited here to an examination of the growth of wages between 1972 and 1976.

Demographic and Work Experience Characteristics

Table 5-6 examines the effects of the demographic characteristics and work experience variables that are used as control variables in the subsequent analysis on the change in wages between 1972 and 1976 for women employed at both dates. Years of schooling and socioeconomic background (measured by father's education), both of which strongly influenced 1972 wages, do not affect the subsequent growth of wages. On the other hand, while neither marriage nor the presence of a young child in 1972 depressed 1972 wages, women with a young child in 1972 experienced an increase in wages over the period that was 42 cents an hour less than that of other women. Women who underwent a change in marital status—whether from married to unmarried or from unmarried to married—experienced a gain in wages substantially below that of women who were married

Table 5-6   Effect of Demographic Characteristics and Work Experience on the Change in Wages between 1972 and 1976 for White Women Employed at Both Dates, Gap ≥ 3 (t-statistics in parentheses)

Variable	Change in Wages
Early 40s, 1976	14.503
	(0.954)
Early 50s, 1976	−5.108
	(−0.402)
Good health, 1972	15.588
	(0.867)

Table 5-6 (continued)

Variable	Change in Wages
Years of schooling	2.351
	(0.842)
Father has 10 or more years of schooling	5.060
	(0.402)
Change in marital status:[a]	-55.144
No husband to husband	(-1.753)*
Change in marital status:[a]	-39.183
Husband to no husband	(-1.719)*
No change in marital status:[a]	-16.090
No husband to no husband	(-0.996)
Child under 6 years of age, 1972	-41.748
	(-1.339)*
Child 6–17 years of age, 1972	28.700
	(1.583)
Years worked 6 months or more through 1967	-0.152
	(-0.136)
Weeks worked 1968–1972	-0.060
	(-0.511)
Weeks worked in last year, 1974	0.710
	(1.600)*
Weeks worked in last year, 1976	1.176
	(2.913)***
Change in hours:[b]	2.050
Full-time to part-time	(0.084)
Change in hours:[b]	48.279
Part-time to full-time	(2.331)**
No change in hours:[b]	29.232
Full-time to full-time	(1.968)**
Resides in South, 1972	2.137
	(0.944)
Local labor force numbers less than 300,000	-14.272
	(-1.283)*
Constant	-57.929
	(-1.270)
Mean Value	98
N	307
R^2	0.167
F	3.022***

[a] Reference category: No change in marital status, married with husband present in 1972 and 1976.

[b] Reference category: No change in hours, worked part time in 1972 and 1976.

*** $p < .01$, ** $p < .05$, * $p < .10$

in both years. Work experience affected not only 1972 wages, but wage growth between 1972 and 1976 as well. The number of weeks worked during the 1972–1976 period had a positive effect on the change in wages over that period, with the number of weeks worked in the year preceding the 1976 interview having the most important effect. Work experience prior to 1972, however, did not affect the change in wages. Furthermore, compared to women who remained in part-time jobs over the period, women who moved from part-time to full-time employment experienced a wage gain that was 48 cents an hour larger, and women who remained in full-time employment experienced a wage gain that was 29 cents larger. It should be recalled that women who worked full time in 1972 earned 16 cents an hour more than those who worked part time. The larger wage gain for those who went from part-time to full-time work suggests that by making the transition to full-time employment these women were able to catch up. Finally, Southern women fared no differently than those who lived elsewhere, while the wage gains of women residing in small labor markets were depressed somewhat.

Effect of Industry and Occupation on Wage Gain

The set of demographic and work experience variables just discussed was much more effective in explaining wages in 1972 than in explaining the change in wages over the following four years.* (This can be seen by comparing the R^2 and F statistics in Tables 5-1 and 5-6.) While a full exploration of the determinants of wage growth among this group of women is outside the scope of this study, the literature on the sex segregation of occupations and the relationship of this phenomenon to the low level and slow advance in women's wages[18] suggests the inclusion of industry and occupation variables in any analysis of the change in their wages.† We considered this issue briefly. Table 5-7 reports the results of adding broad categories

---

* It should be observed that the period under consideration includes the recession years 1973 to 1975. Thus it is possible that the effects of the recession may have confounded the effects of demographic and work experience variables.

† Industry and occupation variables are not included in the cross-sectional analyses of the determinants of 1972 wages and prestige. Preparation for work is translated into higher earnings and/or status through differential access to jobs in industries and occupations with higher pay and/or prestige. It would, therefore, introduce serious problems of multicollinearity if industry and occupation variables were included in the analysis of the effects of activities undertaken in preparation for work on wages and prestige.

Table 5-7   Net Effects of Industry Group and Occupation Group on the Change
in Wages between 1972 and 1976 for White Women Employed at Both
Dates,[a] Gap ≥ 3 (t-statistics in parentheses)

Industry or Occupation	Change in Wages	Mean
Industry, 1972 (reference category: wholesale and retail trade)		
Professional services	14.678 (0.942)	0.35
Other services	−4.570 (−0.135)	0.03
Manufacturing, mining, construction, agriculture	21.087 (1.264)	0.26
Public administration, public utilities, finance, insurance, real estate	41.054 (2.218)***	0.17
Industry, 1976 (reference category: wholesale and retail trade)		
Professional services	22.857 (1.511)*	0.35
Other services	−0.078 (−0.003)	0.04
Manufacturing, mining, construction, agriculture	32.939 (2.011)**	0.24
Public administration, public utilities, finance, insurance, real estate	65.439 (3.713)***	0.17
Occupation, 1972 (reference category: clerical)		
Professional, technical, managerial	9.046 (0.580)	0.18
Other occupation	−18.149 (−1.400)*	0.36
Occupation, 1976 (reference category: clerical)		
Professional, technical, managerial	6.864 (0.443)	0.18
Other occupation	−20.014 (−1.592)*	0.38
Change in Industry 1972–1976 (reference category: same industry)		
Better industry	24.054 (0.976)	0.06
Worse industry	−43.672 (−1.894)**	0.06

Table 5-7   (continued)

Industry or Occupation	Change in Wages	Mean
Change in Occupation 1972–1976		
(reference category: same occupation)		
Better occupation	9.432	0.08
	(0.480)	
Worse occupation	−5.798	0.09
	(−0.299)	
Prestige Status of 1972 Job	1.135	47.51
	(2.112)**	

[a] In all cases multiple regression techniques have been used to control for individual differences in age, health status, education, father's education, presence of children in 1972, change in marital status 1972–1976, years of work experience through 1967, weeks of work experience 1968–1972, weeks of work experience 1974, weeks of work experience 1976, change in hours worked 1972–1976, region of residence 1972, size of local labor force 1972.
*** p < .01, ** p < .05, * p < .10

of industry and occupation to the demographic and work experience variables in the wage-change equation. Three alternative specifications were introduced: 1972 industry or occupation, 1976 industry or occupation, and change in industry or occupation over the period. The industries have been divided into five groups: (1) professional services; (2) public administration, public utilities, finance, insurance, and real estate; (3) manufacturing, mining, construction and agriculture; (4) retail and wholesale trade; and (5) other services. Retail and wholesale trade is the reference category. Occupations have been divided into three groups: (1) professional, technical, and managerial, (2) clerical, and (3) other occupations. As Table 5-7 indicates, women employed in industry group (2)—public administration, public utilities, finance, insurance, or real estate—at either the beginning or the end of the period register substantially larger wage gains than women in other industries. Women who finished the 1972–1976 period in industry groups (1) or (3) also experienced larger wage gains. With respect to occupation group, we find that beginning or ending the period in an occupation other than clerical or professional, technical, or managerial reduced the wage gain by about 18 to 20 cents an hour.

Although the overall distribution of women in our sample by either industry or occupation exhibits no change over the four-year period 1972 to 1976 (see Table 5-7), there was nevertheless movement by individual women. Six percent of the women moved to jobs in "better" *industries* (operationalized as a movement from a higher to a lower numbered industry group), while another 6 percent moved to jobs in "worse" industries. Movement to a job in a "worse" industry reduced the wage gain between 1972 and 1976 by 44 cents an hour. Again, the 8 percent of the women who moved to "better" *occupations* (operationalized as a movement from a higher to a lower numbered occupation) were offset by the 9 percent who moved to a "worse" occupation. Changing occupations does not, however, appear to have a significant effect on the size of the wage gains made by these women.

Finally, we can consider the impact of prestige status of the 1972 job on subsequent advances in wages. This variable does affect the wage gain over the next four years, with women in higher-status jobs at the beginning of the period registering larger gains.

Post-School Preparation for a Career

We turn now to an examination of the effects of post-school investments in human capital and the effects of attributes of jobs held early in the career on the wage gain between 1972 and 1976. As we saw in Table 5-6, years of schooling, which was such an important determinant of wages in 1972, did not contribute to the growth in wages over the subsequent four years. Tables 5-8 and 5-9 summarize the effects of post-school investments in human capital and of attributes of the last job held prior to leaving the labor force on the change in wages between 1972 and 1976. While all of these variables had a significant impact on wages in 1972, only a few of them affected the change in wages as well. Completing a training program increased the wage gain by 28 cents per hour on the average. Women who completed professional, technical, or managerial programs experienced a gain that was 48 cents an hour greater than the gain made by women who did not complete a training program, while those who completed other, nonclerical programs experienced a gain that was 19 cents an hour greater. Obtaining a certificate increased the wage gain by 33 cents an hour, although here it is those who obtained a trade certificate who experienced the larger gain. Consistent with our findings regarding years of schooling, going back to school for additional courses—whether for a high school diploma, college degree, or just for pleasure—does not affect the change in wages, though, as we saw earlier, these activities had a major effect on 1972 wages. The only characteristic of the last job held prior to withdrawal that affects the change in wages over the 1972-1976 period is the

Table 5-8   **Net Effects of Post-School Investments on the Change in Wages between 1972 and 1976 for White Women Employed at Both Dates, Gap ≥ 3[a] (t-statistics in parentheses)**

Aspect of Post-School Investment	Change in Wages
Training Program Completed by 1972	27.871
	(2.554)**
Type of Training Completed by 1972	
(reference category: no training)	
Professional, technical, managerial	48.154
	(2.299)**
Clerical	10.019
	(0.732)
Other	18.791
	(1.474)*
Length of Training Program Completed	
Months of training through 1967	−0.625
	(−0.822)
Weeks of training 1968–1972	−0.235
	(−0.895)
Certificate Obtained by 1972	33.155
	(2.306)**
Type of Certificate Obtained	
(reference category: no certificate)	
Trade certificate	39.409
	(1.252)
Professional certificate	19.102
	(0.885)
Additional Education Courses	
(reference category: no additional schooling)	
Courses for a high school diploma	10.689
	(0.360)
Courses for a college degree	46.667
	(1.218)
Other schooling	4.935
	(0.251)

[a] In all cases multiple regression techniques have been used to control for individual differences in age, health status, education, father's education, presence of children in 1972, change in marital status 1972–1976, years of work experience through 1967, weeks of work experience 1968–1972, weeks of work experience 1974, weeks of work experience 1976, change in hours worked 1972–1976, region of residence 1972, size of local labor force 1972.

*** $p < .01$, ** $p < .05$, * $p < .10$

Table 5-9   Net Effects of Selected Characteristics of Longest Job Held Prior to Withdrawing from the Labor Force on the Change in Wages between 1972 and 1976 for White Women Employed at Both Dates, Gap ≥ 3[a]

Aspect of Last Job Held	Change in Wages
Median Education in Last Job in 1960	0.429
	(0.995)
Median Income in Last Job in 1960	0.001
	(0.367)
Prestige Status of Last Job	0.875
	(1.448)*
Occupation of Last Job	
(reference category: clerical or sales)	
Professional, technical or managerial	14.590
occupation	(0.769)
Other occupation	−1.410
	(−0.107)

[a] In all cases multiple regression techniques have been used to control for individual differences in age, health status, education, father's education, presence of children in 1972, change in marital status 1972–1976, years of work experience through 1967, weeks of work experience 1968–1972, weeks of work experience 1974, weeks of work experience 1976, change in hours worked 1972–1976, region of residence 1972, size of local labor force 1972.
*** $p < .01$, ** $p < .05$, * $p < .10$

prestige status of the job. Median education of incumbents in the last job, median income of incumbents in the last job, and occupation of the last job—all of which affected 1972 wages—do not have a significant effect on the change on wages.

Summary

The question addressed in this chapter is an empirical one: Do any of the activities in which women engage help to prepare them to return to work after their children are in school? Or, alternatively, given the generally lower wages that women earn and occupational sex segregation, are the outcomes upon re-entry about the same regardless of what individual women have done to prepare themselves? The evidence reported here indicates that despite the serious disadvantage at which these women are placed when their earnings are compared with those of men or even with those of other women in their cohort whose work histories are more continuous, there are important differences in labor market position (measured by wages and prestige status of the job) among these women themselves, and that these differences are related to the preparations they have made for a career. Years of schooling, though not the kinds of courses taken, increased both wages and prestige in 1972. Post-school investments in human capital were also effective in increasing 1972 wages and prestige. Returning to school for additional courses increased prestige in 1972, whatever the nature of the courses. Taking additional courses beyond those needed for a high school diploma also increased wages substantially. Completing a training program paid off in terms of both higher wages and more prestige in 1972, with longer training programs resulting in larger increases in wages and prestige. Obtaining a certificate also resulted in higher wages and more prestige, with a professional certificate having most of the effect on initial wages. However, larger increases in wages in the subsequent period were registered by those who obtained a trade certificate.

Another major influence on the wage and prestige positions of women after they re-enter the labor force is the kinds of jobs they held in the early stages of their working lives, prior to leaving paid employment. Even after controlling for differences in education and socioeconomic background, we found that women who held better jobs before they left also held better jobs after returning.

There is, thus, an important role for vocational guidance to play in helping young women in the early stages of their careers to make decisions that will not penalize them at a later stage in the life cycle. Women who are following more traditional life-styles and staying home until their children have entered school should be encouraged to take advantage of whatever opportunities are available for going to school or participating in training programs. These investments in human capital result in substantially higher wages and prestige after re-entry. Moreover, it should be recognized that it is as important for women who are going to leave paid employment while household responsibilities are heaviest as it is for others in the work force to get into the "right" job cluster at the beginning of their careers. Given the current occupational structure, women are generally at a serious disadvantage in this regard. Our findings point to the importance of affirmative action programs, even for women who plan to stop working after a few years but who may, after all, re-enter the work force subsequently.

Endnotes

1. Anne McDougall, *Going Back to School at 35 and Over*, U.S. Department of Labor, Bureau of Labor Statistics, Special Labor Force Report 204 (1977).
2. See, for example, Gary S. Becker, *Human Capital* (New York: National Bureau of Economic Research, 1964); Glen G. Cain, *Married Women in the Labor Force: An Economic Analysis* (Chicago: University of Chicago Press, 1966); W. Lee Hanson, ed., *Education, Income and Human Capital* (New York: Columbia University Press, 1970); Jacob Mincer, *Schooling, Experience and Earnings* (New York: Columbia University Press, 1974); Theodore W. Schultz, "Capital Formation by Education," *Journal of Political Economy*, 67 (December 1960), pp. 571–583; and Theodore W. Schultz, "Investment in Human Capital," *American Economic Review*, 51 (March 1961), pp. 1–17.
3. See, for example, David M. Gordon, *Theories of Poverty and Underemployment* (Lexington, Mass.: D.C. Heath, 1972); Richard C. Edwards, Michael Reich, and David M. Gordon, eds., *Labor Market Segmentation* (Lexington, Mass.: D.C. Heath, 1975); Christopher Jencks, Marshall Smith, Henry Acland, Mary Jo Bane, David Cohen, Hebert Gintis, Barbara Heyns, and Stephen Michelson, *Inequality: A Reassessment of the Effect of Family and Schooling in America* (New York: Basic Books, Inc., 1972); Samuel Bowles and Herbert Gintis, *Schooling in Capitalist America* (New York: Basic Books, 1976); and Lester C. Thurow, *Generating Inequality* (New York: Basic Books, 1975).
4. Clifford B. Hawley and William T. Bielby, "Research Uses of the National Longitudinal Survey of Data on Mature Women," in *Women's Changing Role at Home and on the Job*, National Commission for Manpower Policy, Special Report No. 26 (Washington, D.C.: U.S. Government Printing Office, September 1978), p. 77.
5. Thurow, *op. cit.*
6. Gordon, *op. cit.*
7. Bowles and Gintis, *op. cit.*
8. C. L. Jusenius and S. H. Sandell, "Barriers to Entry and Re-Entry to the Labor Market," paper presented at the Conference on Research Needed to Improve the Employment and Employability of Women, U.S. Department of Labor, Women's Bureau, Washington, D.C., 1974.
9. R. Koppel and E. Appelbaum, "The Impact of Labor Market Sex Discrimination on the Wages and Earnings of Young Women," paper presented at the meetings of the American Sociological Association, New York City, 1976; D. Shapiro and T. J. Carr, "Investments in Human Capital and the Earnings of Young Women," in F. L. Mott, S. Sandell, D. Shapiro, P. Brito, T. Carr, R. Johnson, C. Jusenius, P. Koenig, and S. Moore, *Years for Decision*, Vol. IV (Washington, D.C.: U.S. Government Printing Office, 1978).
10. Shapiro and Carr, *op. cit.*, p. 161.
11. C. Bose, "Women and Jobs: Sexual Influences on Occupational Prestige," Ph.D. dissertation, Johns Hopkins University, 1973.
12. The probit program eliminates respondents for whom any information required for the analyses reported in Tables 5-2 through 5-5 is missing. This is not true of the ordinary least squares regression analysis. As a result, the number of

women included in the analysis of job satisfaction is smaller than the number included in the analyses of wages and prestige.

13. Bowles and Gintis, *op. cit.*; Thurow, *op. cit.*

14. Shultz, *op. cit.*; Becker, *op. cit.*; Hansen, *op. cit.*; Mincer, *op. cit.*; Otis Dudley Duncan, David L. Featherman, and Beverly Duncan, *Socioeconomic Background and Achievements* (New York: Seminar Press, 1972); and William H. Sewell and Robert M. Hauser, *Education, Occupation, and Earnings* (New York: Academic Press, 1975). For recent statements addressed specifically to the economic achievements of women, see Shapiro and Carr, *op. cit.*; G. G. Cain and M. D. Dooley, "Estimation of a Model of Labor Supply, Fertility and Wages of Married Women," *Journal of Political Economy*, 84 (1976), pp. s179–s199; Donald J. Treiman and Kermit Terrell, "Sex and the Process of Status Achievement: A Comparison of Working Women and Men," *American Sociological Review*, 40 (April 1975), pp. 174–200; and McKee J. McLendon, "Sex and Occupational Status," paper presented at the meetings of the American Sociological Association, San Francisco, 1975.

15. Duncan, Featherman, and Duncan, *op. cit.*; Sewell and Hauser, *op. cit.*; Treiman and Terrell, *op. cit.*; and McLendon, *op. cit.*

16. Nicholas M. Kiefer, "Population Heterogeneity and Inference from Panel Data on the Effects of Vocational Education," *Journal of Political Economy*, 87 (1979), pp. s213–s226.

17. Gordon, *op. cit.*; Edwards, Reich, and Gordon, *op. cit.*

18. Mary H. Stevenson, "Relative Wages and Sex Segregation by Occupation" in Cynthia B. Lloyd, ed., *Sex, Discrimination, and the Division of Labor* (New York: Columbia University Press, 1975); and Francine D. Blau and Carol L. Jusenius, "Economists' Approaches to Sex Segregation in the Labor Market: An Appraisal" in Martha Blaxall and Barbara Reagan, eds., *Women and the Workplace: The Implications of Occupational Segregation* (Chicago: University of Chicago Press, 1976).

Chapter 6

THE CHOICE OF HOURS AND WEEKS OF WORK

While most women who work are employed full time, a sizable minority of working women work less than 35 hours a week or less than 48 weeks a year. Currently, about 34 percent of all employed women in the United States work part of the week, and most of these women work only part of the year as well.[1] For some of these women, part-time employment (part-week or part-year) is involuntary—they would prefer full-time employment but are unable to obtain it. Among white women, however, 84 percent of those who work less than 35 hours a week do so by choice.[2] Moreover, there has been a rapid increase in the number of women seeking to work 34 hours a week or less. About two thirds of the increase in voluntary part-time employment between 1954 and 1977 was accounted for by women, as the proportion of working women rose from 33 to 41 percent of all non-agricultural employees and the proportion of women working part of the week (less than 35 hours a week) voluntarily rose from 16 to 24 percent of all employed women.[3] Despite rapid increases in part-week employment the supply of women who want to work less than a full week has, in fact, increased more rapidly than the demand for such workers, resulting in persistently high unemployment rates. Currently, about 25 percent of all unemployed women are seeking part-week work.[4]

Adult women have frequently sought part-time employment as a means of meeting home and child care responsibilities while contributing to family income. Family and home responsibilities are the most common reasons cited by women for working part of the week[5] or part of the year,[6] though this reason has declined in importance since 1960. Wives with very young children continue to be less likely than other women to work 35 hours a week. In 1979, 37.2 percent of married women with children under the age of three who were employed worked part of the week; while among all employed women the proportion in part-week employment was 28.2 percent.[7]

Part-time employment opportunities have increased rapidly largely as a result of the expansion of retail trade and service industries. The uneven flow of demands in these industries and the fact that consumers often do their shopping, eat at restaurants, and utilize recreation facilities in the evening and on weekends means that firms cannot cover peak activity periods with full-time workers on a standard 9-to-5 shift. Owners and managers in these industries have come to rely on part-week workers to supplement, and sometimes to replace, full-time employees. Adult women, in particular, have proved useful in meeting the need of business for workers on non-standard work schedules. About 70 percent of all adult workers on part-week schedules are women.[8]

Despite the fact that part-week employees fill an important role in such industries, they often do not do as well in the labor market as full-time workers. Fringe benefits often do not apply to part-time employees. More important, part-week workers are often paid less than full-time employees of the same sex, race, and educational level.[9] Yet a substantial minority of working women, constrained by the traditional responsibility for child care and household tasks, continue to seek part-week employment. In this chapter we explore the implications of part-week employment for women returning to work and address the question of what, given the apparently voluntary nature of such employment, are the policy issues.

Preference and Necessity in Determining Hours and Weeks of Work

From the neoclassical perspective, study of the related issues of weeks worked per year and usual hours worked per week is of interest only for the insights it provides for comprehending the household decision-making process and for predicting future trends in labor supply. Study of these issues is not undertaken, even when it is the labor supply of women that is under consideration, with a view toward the development of appropriate public policies to address the special problems of part-year or part-week workers. The reason for this is quite simple: From the neoclassical perspective, there are no special problems associated with part-time work. Women and other workers who are usually employed part time are, it is argued, acting on the basis of preferences with respect to consumption and to leisure (interpreted broadly as nonmarket time available either for direct consumption as leisure or for use in nonmarket activities that contribute to utility) given their own wage rates and all other income available to their households. Dissatisfaction with part-time work is hardly a cause for public intervention in the world of neoclassical economics, since the individual has at hand the obvious remedy: namely, altering the number of annual hours of labor supplied and/or the way they are distributed over weeks until utility is maximized. Especially in those cases where the worker is employed less than full time in terms of either annual hours or weeks of work, the labor supply decision is viewed as reflecting the worker's choice of the preferred combination of annual weeks and hours. Modifications are admitted in the case of full-time workers, who usually face a demand for their services that leaves them only an all-or-nothing choice. Exogenous influences on weeks worked (vacations of mandated length, involuntary layoffs), and even on hours worked, by workers preferring full-time employment are recognized. But such modifications are singularly absent from discussions of part-time work.

In a discussion that is representative of the state of the art in the neoclassical theory of what determines the number of hours and weeks of labor a worker supplies, Giora Hanoch[10] makes quite explicit the assumptions underlying the neoclassical model. A careful reading of his explanations of these underlying assumptions reveals at just what junctures neoclassical writers assume away any role for public policy. Though one might quarrel with several of the neoclassical assumptions, we shall limit ourselves here to the two that are most inimical to an understanding of the labor supply decisions of women and that, not coincidentally, imply that public policy is largely irrelevant.

Exogenous Constraints on Hours of Work

The first tenet of the neoclassical approach with which we wish to take issue is the overarching view that exogenous influences do not affect the labor supply choices of part-time workers. Where women, in particular, are concerned, there is one major exogenous factor

affecting labor supply that would seem inescapable—the availability
of child care. Yet discussions of child care, either as a constraint on
employment or in relation to fertility decisions is conspicuously absent from that body of literature that has come to be called "the new
home economics." Perhaps the high employment rate for mothers of
young children has led these home economists to assume that nearly
all such mothers who want to work are able to arrange satisfactory
child care without much difficulty. A recent study by two sociologists
of the bearing of child care on the work and fertility nexus,[11] however, affirms that absence of satisfactory child care is, in fact, an
important (exogenous) constraint on weeks and hours of work for
mothers with children under age five. In their analysis of a national
sample of mothers of young children, the authors of this study found
that among those not in the labor force, one in six would choose to
work if they could arrange satisfactory child care; while among
mothers employed part time, one in four felt they were prevented
from working more hours by the unavailability of suitable child care.
In the neoclassical framework, where no allowance is made for the
prevalence of a child-care constraint on hours and weeks worked,
this lack of adequate child care appears as the mother's preference
for nonmarket activities.

The availability of day care for preschool children is the most
obvious restriction on hours and weeks of labor supplied by women,
but it is certainly not the only such constraint. Whatever their *preferences* with respect to hours and weeks of work, the work schedules
of mothers are constrained by the paucity of after-school and
school-vacation activities (including transportation to such activities),
by the virtual non-existence of infirmaries to care for mildly sick
children and of routine dental and medical care in school for well
children, as well as by a total lack of communal kitchens and similar
support facilities. The lack of reliable public transportation, characteristic of most parts of the United States, places a further exogenous
constraint on hours worked.

Part-time workers are subject to another important type of
exogenous influence on hours and weeks worked, this one very
similar to the kinds of factors that restrict the ability of full-time
workers to freely choose to supply the utility-maximizing combination of weeks and hours. The growth of part-time employment has
paralleled the growth of retail trade and service industries. The
reason for this is that goods can be produced at an even pace and
held in inventories to meet demand, whereas services can't be in-

ventoried but must be provided on demand. When demand is uneven, or must be met for extended hours on weekends or during the
evening, employers favor part-time employment as a means of
fitting the work force to the work load. It follows that workers seeking part-time work will be constrained to work during those hours of
the week and during those weeks of the year when demand is high,
facing involuntary layoffs during the off-season. Weekly hours may
also be influenced by seasonal factors. The large number of voluntary part-time workers employed in wholesale and retail trade—
34.1 million voluntary workers employed in these industries in 1978
out of a total of 90.5 million voluntary part-time wage and salary
workers[12]—suggests that such exogenous influences on weekly as
well as annual hours of labor supplied may not be trivial.

Interaction of Wages and Hours of Work

The observation that part-time work is concentrated in particular
occupations and industries leads us to our second, and perhaps more
vehement, objection to the assumptions on which the neoclassical
theory of labor supply is based. In explaining the assumptions underlying the neoclassical model of labor supply, Hanoch[13] writes
that the model assumes perfect substitutability of hours of work from
the point of view of the *demand* for labor. That is, the wage rate is
assumed independent of total hours $A = KH$, as well as of their
allocation between K and H (A = annual workhours, K = weeks
worked per year, H = hours worked per workweek). Existing evidence suggests, however, that this assumption is entirely unwar-
ranted. One major study of part-time employment that included
extensive interviews with managers and employers who utilize part-
time workers found that managers and employers generally hold a
number of negative attitudes toward these employees.[14] The study
found that part-time workers are believed to have less frequent
long-range career plans and to be less interested in their jobs. It also
found that stereotypes about low-level jobs, which are often held by
part-time workers, negatively affect managers' perceptions about all
part-time workers. Moreover, the study found that some companies
have explicit policies against promotion for part-time workers, and
that other policies as well may create status differences between
part- and full-time workers. In addition to these negative attitudes
toward part-time workers, employers generally hold the view that
jobs involving continuous-process technologies are not suited to

part-time employment. These include, in particular, jobs in manufacturing industries—in which only 5.9 percent of all employees
were on voluntary part-time schedules in 1978;[15] and employment
in supervisory, management, and executive occupations—in which
only 3.3 percent of all employees in 1977 usually worked part time
voluntarily.[16] Employers are reluctant to hire part-time employees
for these jobs because the work to be performed requires continuity.
On the other hand, job technologies involving discrete tasks, repetitive, tedious, or stressful work, are believed by managers and employers to be particularly well-suited to part-time employment. All
of this suggests that the really good jobs are not open to part-time
workers, and that there may be a high concentration of part-time
employees in industries and occupations where all workers are
poorly paid. In addition, Nollen *et al.*[17] found that employers tend to
view part-time work as a labor cost-reduction strategy. In part, this
is accomplished by substituting part-time workers for overtime work
by full-time employees; but part-time employment is also used to
reduce labor costs by paying part-time workers less than full-time
workers and by excluding them from some or all fringe benefits.

Far from being independent of total annual hours or hours worked
per week, as Hanoch assumes, the wage rate an individual with
given skills and productivity characteristics can command may be
systematically related to whether he or she works full or part time,
since choosing part-time work may exclude a worker from the better
jobs. In the determination of the wages of part-time workers, individual productivity characteristics may be dominated by the characteristics of jobs for which employers are willing to hire them. That
this is, in fact, the case is the conclusion reached in another study
concerned with why hourly earnings are lower for part-time than for
full-time workers.[18] The results reported in that study indicate that
part-time workers earn less, in part, because some employers do pay
part-time employees less for the same work. But the main reason for
the wage gap between part-time and full-time employees, the study
found, is that part-time workers are relegated to the lower-paid
sectors of the economy. In analyzing the wages of full-time and
part-time workers by sector, using 10 broad industry and 20 broad
occupation categories, the study found that about two thirds of the
wage gap resulted from the fact that part-time workers are concentrated in sectors where pay is generally lower.

Part-Time Jobs and Women's Skills

Analysis of the occupational and industrial distribution of women on part-time schedules has consistently shown that most part-time employment is in jobs that are either routine or unskilled.[19] Currently, among women who work part time, nearly two thirds are clerical or nonprofessional service workers. Only about 12 percent hold professional or technical jobs, and most of the rest are employed as sales workers. Women who work part time and hold jobs at the higher end of the occupational distribution (about one eighth of the part-time women workers) are trained as nurses, teachers, medical technicians, dieticians, or social workers.[20] However, even part-time jobs in their fields for professional or semiprofessional women are likely to be nonprofessional or quasi-professional in nature. The actual tasks performed may not even be related to the profession. Professional and semiprofessional women "employed on a part-time basis are likely to be placed in the lower and more undesirable positions in the organization when they are employed, and they often receive salaries which are below their level of intelligence and competence."[21] Moreover, "[t]here are usually no administrative responsibilities in these professional jobs."[22] As for the distribution by industry, part-time employment, while found in all industries, is presently concentrated in wholesale and retail trade and in service industries. In 1978 more than a third of all employees in wholesale and retail trade were on part-time schedules, as were nearly half of all employees in the finance and service sectors.[23] Detailed information on part-time employment by industry indicates that the specific industries in which one third or more of the women work part time are: agriculture services; wholesale trade of farm products; retail trade establishments including food stores, drug stores, department stores, and eating and drinking places; real estate; business services such as employment agencies; all personal services including private household; religious organizations; and non-profit membership organizations.[24] In the public administration industry, where many of the better jobs are to be found, part-time employment has lagged behind. In the federal government the proportion of part-time employment, except in the postal service, is far below that in the private sector.[25] While part-time employment in civil service positions increased between 1977 and 1979, part-time employees were still less than 3 percent of all federal employees in 1979.[26]

The unequal distribution of part-time employment of women across industries reflects the distribution of skilled and unskilled jobs within these industries. Women in part-time jobs are concentrated in occupations in which skill requirements are low and in the industries in which such occupations are found. Owen's study for the Department of Labor is significant in this regard because it has gone beyond profiling the characteristics of part-time employment.[27] Utilizing multivariate analysis to control for individual differences in education and work experience as well as in demographic characteristics, Owen concluded that part-time workers are concentrated in the low-wage sectors of the economy despite the diversity in their backgrounds.

Thus the evidence indicates that for a woman who accepts part-time employment, whether because this is the allocation of time she prefers or because exogenous constraints on her use of time dictate this choice, the decision to work part time is likely to result in a lower-paying job. It is quite clear, the assumptions of the neoclassical model of female labor supply aside, that part-time and full-time work are *not* perfect substitutes from the point of view of the *demand* for labor; and the wage rate cannot be assumed independent of either hours worked per week or weeks worked per year. In almost direct contrast to the neoclassical vision, in which the wage a worker can command is related only to his or her productivity characteristics (and hence is independent of hours worked), it is evident that the labor market is segmented and that part-time workers are unable to compete for jobs on an equal basis with similarly qualified full-time workers. Owen has suggested the use of the job competition model[28] rather than the neoclassical model, in order to explain wage determination for part-time workers:[29]

> It is useful here to picture the labor market as consisting of queues of applicants ranked by quality and lists of jobs ranked by skill level and wages, with the market matching people and jobs with greater or lesser success. One can then think of part-timers and full-timers as composing two separate but overlapping queues. Within each queue, workers are ranked by personal characteristics, but between queues, full-timers are generally ranked ahead of part-timers. Part-timers can compete with full-timers for high-paid jobs only when they have a distinct edge in education, experience, and other personal characteristics that help to predict job performance and training costs.

While this model predicts that the wages of part-time workers will vary on the basis of their individual characteristics, it also predicts that a part-time worker will generally be hired for a job requiring less skill and paying lower wages than a full-time worker of equal qualifications and ability. Moreover, it very clearly predicts that wages are not independent of the number of hours worked per week.

Implications for Women Returning to Work

In terms of hours and weeks of work, the women in our sample conform quite closely to the statistics reported for all working women in the United States. Thirty-three percent of the women in our sample who were employed in 1976 worked less than 35 hours per week (Table 6-1), while among all working women in 1976 the proportion who worked part of the week was about 34 percent.[30] A somewhat higher proportion of the women in our sample who work part of the week do so on a year-round basis: about 44 percent of these women as compared with 33 percent of all working women.[31] Still, most of the women who work part of the week work only part of the year.

Important differences can be seen in the distributions by industry of full-week and part-week workers (Table 6-2). Among women returning to work after a lapse of three or more years, those who worked part of the week in 1972 or 1976 were twice as likely to be employed in wholesale or retail trade or in personal services as those who worked a full week. Conversely, part-week workers were only half as likely to be employed in public administration and only one third as likely to be employed in manufacturing as women who worked a full week. The occupational distributions of full-week and part-week workers are reported in Table 6-3. Both part-week and full-week workers are heavily represented in the clerical occupa-

Table 6-1 Hours per Week by Weeks Worked per Year, 1976 (White Women, Gap ≥ 3)

	Weeks Worked per Year			
Hours per Week	Total (percent)	1–26 (percent)	27–47 (percent)	48–52 (percent)
1–34	33.0	19.8	36.5	43.7
35 or more	67.0	6.5	18.9	74.6
N	506	55	125	326

Table 6-2   Women at Work by Full-Week or Part-Week Status and by Industry,
1972 and 1976 (White Women, Gap ≥ 3)

Industry	Part-Week		Full-Week	
	1972 *(percent)*	1976 *(percent)*	1972 *(percent)*	1976 *(percent)*
Agriculture	0.7	0.6	0.7	0.8
Goods-producing	9.7	9.9	30.7	26.9
Mining	0.0	0.0	0.0	0.0
Construction	1.4	1.1	0.3	2.2
Manufacturing	8.3	8.8	30.4	24.7
Service-producing	89.6	89.5	68.6	72.3
Transportation, communication, and public utilities	4.2	1.7	3.0	3.1
Wholesale and retail trade	29.9	32.6	15.9	16.9
Finance, insurance, and real estate	6.9	6.1	8.1	8.4
Business and repair services	0.7	2.2	1.4	1.7
Personal services	5.6	6.6	2.0	2.5
Entertainment and recreation services	0.7	0.0	0.0	0.6
Professional and related services	38.9	36.5	32.4	30.6
Public administration	2.1	3.3	5.4	7.9
N	143	180	295	354

Note: Percentages may not add to 100 due to rounding.

tions, with more than two fifths of the women in each category in
such occupations. However, part-week workers were twice as likely
to be employed as private household or other service workers as
were full-week workers: 25.4 percent as compared with 12.3 percent
in 1976. In addition, part-week workers were nearly four times as
likely to be employed in sales occupations as were full-week workers
in 1976, with 15.5 percent of part-week workers holding such jobs
compared with 4.2 percent of full-week workers. While part-week
workers were nearly as likely to be employed as professional or
technical workers as full-week workers in 1972, this was no longer
true in 1976. In 1976 12.6 percent of full-week workers were employed in professional or technical positions as compared with only
6.1 percent of part-week workers. Full-week workers were also
twice as likely as part-week workers to be employed as managers and
officials, and nearly three times as likely as part-week workers to be
employed as craftsmen or operatives.

Table 6-3   Women at Work by Full-Week or Part-Week Status and by Occupation, 1972 and 1976 (White Women, Gap ⩾ 3)

	Part-Week		Full-Week	
Occupation	1972 (percent)	1976 (percent)	1972 (percent)	1976 (percent)
Professional and technical	10.4	6.1	12.5	12.6
Managers and officials	2.1	2.8	6.1	5.6
Clerical	47.9	42.5	43.2	44.9
Sales	9.0	15.5	3.7	4.2
Craftsmen	0.7	0.6	2.7	2.2
Operatives	7.6	6.1	20.6	15.7
Private household	2.8	3.3	0.3	1.1
Service	19.4	22.1	9.5	11.2
Farm laborers	0.0	0.6	0.0	0.6
Laborers	0.0	0.6	1.0	0.8
N	144	181	295	353

Note: Percentages may not add to 100 due to rounding.

As we saw in the previous chapter (see Table 5-1), weeks worked and hours worked both affected hourly earnings in 1972. In addition, weeks worked affected the prestige status of the 1972 job. Controlling for individual differences in both demographic characteristics and work-related characteristics, we found a small but significant difference in wages between full-week and part-week workers amounting to 16 cents an hour in 1972. For women who worked in both 1972 and 1976, however, we found that the wage gain over that period was strongly influenced by hours worked per week. Thus Table 5-6 shows that women who went from part-week to full-week work experienced an increase in hourly wages that was 48 cents larger than women who remained in part-week work. Women employed as full-week workers in 1972 who continued to work a full week in 1976 experienced an increase in hourly wages that was 29 cents larger than those employed part of the week at both dates. These differences are net of the effects of individual differences in demographic or other work experience characteristics. Annual weeks of work were also an important influence on the size of the wage gain. Women who worked year round in the year preceding the 1976 survey experienced a wage gain of almost 30 cents an hour more than those who worked only 26 weeks.

The arguments put forth in the preceding section of this chapter suggest that the striking wage gains for women who moved from

Table 6-4   Change in Industry and/or Occupation by Change in Hours Between
1972 and 1976 (White Women, Gap ≥ 3)

		Change in Industry (%)	
Change in Hours	Change in Occupation	No Change	Change
Part week to full week	No change	55.6	22.2
	Change	8.3	13.9
Part week to part week	No change	67.5	5.2
	Change	18.2	9.1
Full week to full week	No change	72.3	8.0
	Change	13.4	6.3
Full week to part week	No change	33.3	19.0
	Change	9.5	38.1

part-time to full-time employment probably resulted from a change
in industry or occupation. Table 6-4 confirms that women who move
from part-week to full-week employment are, in fact, much more
likely to change occupation or industry or both than women who
remain in either part-week or full-week employment. About 44 percent of those increasing hours also changed one-digit industry and/or
occupation category as compared with about 32 percent of those
remaining in part-week employment and 28 percent of those remaining in full-week jobs. The greatest change of all was experienced by women who went from full-week to part-week jobs, 67
percent of whom changed industry or occupation.

The evidence in Chapter 5 suggests that women working part of the
week in 1972 were doing almost as well as those working a full
week, but that their relative situation declined between 1972 and
1976. The reasons for that decline can be addressed more directly by
stratifying our sample by part-week or full-week status, and examining the extent to which hourly earnings are related to education
and work experience. This is done in Table 6-5. All of the human
capital (education and work experience) variables are highly
significant predictors of wages for women employed 35 hours a week
or more. This was true in both 1972 and 1976. Among women who
worked part of the week in 1972, education and recent work experience again had highly significant effects on wages, though work
experience through 1967 did not. By 1976, however, years of
schooling, which in 1972 was the strongest influence on wages,
failed to achieve significance. Neither education nor recent work
experience had a significant effect on the wages of part-week workers in 1976, although wages were influenced by earlier work experience. Moreover, the wage equation for part-week workers in 1976

Table 6-5   Effect of Demographic Characteristics and Work Experience on the Wages of Part-Week and Full-Week Workers, 1972 and 1976 (White Women, Gap ≥ 3) (t-statistics in parentheses)

Variable	Part-Week		Full-Week	
	1972	1976	1972	1976
Late 30s, 1972	17.257	2.131	−2.842	4.761
	(0.745)	(0.104)	(−0.185)	(0.238)
Late 40s, 1972	2.629	−4.204	12.643	−11.997
	(0.125)	(−0.202)	(0.960)	(−0.674)
Years of schooling	18.013	4.239	17.058	21.605
	(3.644)***	(0.885)	(6.491)***	(6.376)***
Husband present	63.608	45.623	2.168	19.446
	(2.218)**	(1.678)*	(0.155)	(1.102)
Child under 6 years of age	94.706	a	4.614	a
	(1.740)*		(0.158)	
Child 6–17 years of age	42.840	a	−13.191	a
	(1.027)		(−0.855)	
Child present	a	25.991	a	−16.832
		(1.071)		(−0.963)
Years worked 6 months or more through 1967	2.159	2.556	2.868	2.719
	(1.058)	(1.318)*	(2.681)***	(1.738)**
Weeks worked 1968–1972	0.338	0.128	0.442	0.294
	(2.395)***	(1.065)	(3.509)***	(2.489)***
Weeks worked 1974	a	0.535	a	1.198
		(1.131)		(2.371)***
Weeks worked 1976	a	0.875	a	1.447
		(1.771)**		(2.669)***
Local labor force numbers less than 400,000	−22.935	−12.149	−43.277	−72.690
	(−1.253)	(−0.638)	(−3.731)***	(−4.645)***
Constant	−155.413	104.847	15.026	−7.814
	(−1.314)	(1.366)	(0.389)	(−0.150)
Mean value (cents)	250	286	285	378
N	121	140	269	292
R^2	0.248	0.132	0.266	0.299
F	4.060	1.963	10.403	11.982

[a] Variable not in this regression.

*** $p < .01$, ** $p < .05$, * $p < .10$

provides a much poorer fit to the data than do the other wage equations.

The ratio of the wages of women working part of the week in 1972 to those of women working a full week was 88 percent. In 1976 the wages of part-week workers amounted to only 76 percent of those of full-week workers. The relative position of part-week workers deteriorated over the four-year period. Moreover, the wages of part-week workers in 1976, unlike those of full-week workers at both dates or of part-week workers in 1972, were not affected by individual differences in investments in human capital. Surprisingly, even years of schooling had no effect on the wages of women working part time in 1976. This finding differs substantially from that of Owen, who reported[32]

> [T]he average hourly wage of the part-time worker is substantially below that of the full-time worker, but among part-timers, economic rewards vary on the basis of personal characteristics in much the same way as do the wages of full-time workers.

The difference in findings is probably attributable to the fact that Owen's study is based on 1973 data. Our findings for 1972 are quite close to his for 1973. By 1976, however, economic rewards to part-week workers in our sample no longer varied with individual differences in human capital. A comparison of the occupational distribution of part-week workers in 1972 with the distribution in 1976 (Table 6-3) suggests that by 1976 such workers were locked even more firmly into the low-wage sectors of the economy. Most noticeably, the proportion holding professional and technical positions declined from 10.4 percent of part-week workers in 1972 to 6.1 percent in 1976, while the proportion holding sales positions increased from 9.0 percent to 15.5 percent over the same period. Further support for the argument that the labor market has become increasingly segmented, with part-week workers relegated to low-skill, low-paying jobs regardless of their individual qualifications, is provided by the finding that 1976 wages of these workers did not vary with education or recent work experience.

Thus there have been substantial economic disadvantages associated with part-time work for women re-entering the labor force after an absence of several years, a situation which worsened over the period 1972 to 1976.

Conclusion

Returning to work as part-week workers had serious negative economic repercussions for the women in our sample. Average wages for these women, as we have seen, were considerably below those for women who worked 35 hours or more per week. The evidence suggests that women re-entering the work force face a segmented labor market in which women who work part of the week are unable to compete for the better jobs with women who work a full week. In general part-week jobs are available in sectors of the economy in which all workers are poorly paid. By 1976 the characteristics of the jobs available to part-week workers in our sample dominated any individual differences in human capital among these workers, and economic rewards did not vary with schooling or work experience.

The failure of years of schooling to affect 1976 wages for part-week workers suggests that the differential cannot be narrowed by further investments in human capital by these workers. There is no reason to think that the better jobs, which might require such additional skills, will be available to women working less than 35 hours a week. The rapid increase in the numbers of women willing to accept part-week work, whether because this is the allocation of time that maximizes their utility or as a result of exogenous constraints on the use of their time, leaves firms with little incentive to improve the quality of jobs available to such workers. Given the current structure of the labor market, the decision to work fewer than 35 hours a week greatly increases the likelihood that a woman will be under-employed in the sense that the jobs available to her will not utilize her skills or reward them appropriately. The wage she can command in the market is thus not independent of the number of hours a week that she works. Public policies to improve the economic situation of part-week workers are difficult to formulate, since no improvement is likely unless the structure of the labor market is altered to upgrade the quality of jobs available to them. This would require the restructuring of jobs that are usually held by men in order to provide improved opportunities for part-week work. Such a change would attract women to non-traditional fields and would, at the same time, open up the possibility for men to work fewer hours without loss of status or a disproportionate loss of income.

As Barrett points out, "there are compelling social and economic reasons for improving the job market prospects of part-time workers and for eliminating the economic penalties connected with hiring and being hired for part-time work."[33] Women who work part time are not primarily wives working intermittently for "pin money." Married women working part time are, increasingly, women with a permanent commitment to the labor force whose families depend on their incomes. Other women seeking part-time employment are household heads and mothers for whom the availability of a part-time job spells the difference between work and welfare. For these women, fringe benefits for part-time work—especially health and hospitalization insurance—may be crucial to the choice of work or welfare, since welfare recipients are eligible for free medical care under the Medicaid program. Improvement of the part-time job market to make well-paying, part-time employment available should be an important element of programs designed to promote equal employment opportunity for men and women—and of programs designed to reduce the welfare rolls. It would also permit a general reallocation of hours of work inside and outside the home for husbands and wives. An immediate step that should be taken is the elimination of disincentives to employers to provide part-time work (for example, employer contributions to Social Security are higher for two part-time employees earning $15,000 each than for one full-time employee earning $30,000).

Identifying and removing exogenous constraints that limit the amount of hours and weeks of labor a woman supplies would, the evidence suggests, also result in a major improvement in the position of women who now work part of the week or part of the year. Substantial wage gains were experienced by women who went from part-week employment in 1972 to full-week employment in 1976. Similarly, increases in the number of weeks worked per year also significantly affected the wage gain over that period. While recognizing that such constraints as the limited availability of the child care and the deficiencies in public transportation are not easily or quickly removed, we must nevertheless insist that it is time now for the United States to make the investments in infrastructure that will enable women to participate more fully in the economy.

Endnotes

1. *Employment and Training Report of the President* (1980), Table B–14.
2. William V. Deuterman, Jr. and Scott Campbell Brown, "Voluntary Part Time Workers: A Growing Part of the Labor Force," *Monthly Labor Review, 101* (June 1978), pp. 3–10.
3. *Ibid.*
4. *Ibid.*
5. *Ibid.*
6. U.S. Department of Labor, Bureau of Labor Statistics, *Perspectives on Working Women,* Bulletin 2080 (October 1980), Table 20.
7. *Ibid.,* Table 28.
8. U.S. Department of Commerce, Bureau of the Census, *Statistical Portrait of Women in the U.S.: 1978,* Current Population Reports, Series P-23, No. 100 (February 1980), Table 6.7.

9. John D. Owen, "Why Part-Time Workers Tend to Be in Low Wage Jobs," *Monthly Labor Review, 101* (June 1978), pp. 11–14.
10. Giora Hanoch, "Hours and Weeks in the Theory of Labor Supply" in James P. Smith, ed., *Female Labor Supply: Theory and Estimation* (Princeton, N.J.: Princeton University Press, 1980).
11. Harriet B. Presser and Wendy Baldwin, "Child Care as a Constraint on Employment: Prevalence, Correlates and Bearing on the Work and Fertility Nexus," *American Journal of Sociology,* 85 (March 1980), pp. 1202–1213.
12. U.S. Department of Labor, Bureau of Labor Statistics, *Employment and Earnings* (June 1978), p. 42.
13. Hanoch, *op. cit.*
14. Stanley D. Nollen, Brenda Broz Eddy, and Virginia Hider Martin, *Permanent Part-Time Employment* (New York: Praeger Special Studies, 1978).
15. *Employment and Earnings, op. cit.*
16. Deuterman and Brown, *op. cit.*
17. Nollen, *et al., op. cit.*
18. Owen, *op. cit.*
19. Nollen *et al., op cit.*
20. *Ibid.*
21. A. Theodore, "The Professional Woman: Trends and Prospects" in A. Theodore, ed., *The Professional Woman* (Cambridge, Mass.: Schenkman Publishing Company, 1971), p. 26.
22. Nollen *et al., op. cit.*, p. 13.
23. *Employment and Earnings, op. cit.*
24. Carol Leon and Robert W. Bednarzik, "A Profile of Women on Part-Time Schedules," *Monthly Labor Review, 101* (October 1978), pp. 3–12.
25. Nollen, *et al., op. cit.*
26. *Employment and Training Report of the President* (1979), p. 87. New legislation, the Federal Employees Part-Time Career Employment Act of 1978 (Public Law 95-437), eliminates two major obstacles to the hiring of part-time employees and is expected to result in more part-time job opportunities with the federal government.
27. Owen, *op. cit.*
28. Lester C. Thurow, *Generating Inequality* (New York: Basic Books, 1975).
29. Owen, *op. cit.*, p. 13.
30. *Employment and Training Report of the President* (1980), Table B-14.
31. *Ibid.*
32. Owen, *op. cit.*, p. 14.
33. Nancy S. Barrett, "Women in the Job Market: Unemployment and Work Schedules" in Ralph E. Smith, ed., *The Subtle Revolution: Women at Work* (Washington, D.C.: The Urban Institute, 1979), p. 87.

Chapter 7

THE EMPLOYMENT OF MARRIED WOMEN: TRENDS AND PROSPECTS

Economists have been notoriously unsuccessful in predicting the participation of married women in the labor force. The difficulty lies chiefly in a faulty analysis of female labor supply decisions. Standard economic explanations are based on a model that casts the question of the labor force participation of married women in terms of each individual woman's decision with respect to the allocation of her time between work at home, paid employment, and leisure. Economists argue that there are two opposing forces set in motion by rising real wages that affect this decision. A rise in family income as husbands' real wages increase induces an "income effect" in which women choose leisure or work within the home over paid employment. Conversely, rising real wages for women induce a "substitution effect," causing women to substitute paid employment for unpaid work at home or for leisure-time activities, thus increasing their participation in the labor force. It follows as a corollary to the substitution effect that the presence of young children in the family increases the value of a woman's time spent in the home and thus reduces the likelihood that a married woman with young children will work.

It is not easy to reconcile this theoretical model with the behavior of women in the aggregate since World War II. Thus, despite the steady increase in husbands' real wages and the consequent rapid growth in family income, increases in the labor force participation rate for married women during the 1950s and early 1960s consistently exceeded the expectations and predictions of economists. Holding firmly to their model of how women ought to behave, however, the economists were undaunted. They boldly concluded *ex post* that events had demonstrated that the substitution effect outweighed the income effect in influencing the decision by women to seek paid work. Women, they reasoned, were not making a simple leisure versus labor decision, but were also choosing between a paying job and unpaid work at home. Rising real wages for women attracted them into paid activities within the labor market by providing the family with additional income sufficient to permit a "reduction in unpaid work through the purchase of labor-saving devices, restaurant service, and the like."[1] As economists perceived what was happening, women were not substituting paid work for leisure. They were substituting it for unpaid work at home. Unfortunately for the economists, studies done in the 1960s of the use of time by married women who worked do not confirm this view. The Walker and Woods study of time use[2] carried out in 1967–1968 found that wives who were employed full time devoted an average of 71 hours per week to paid and unpaid work, wives who were employed part time spent 65 hours per week in work activities, while wives who were primarily homemakers devoted a total of 60 hours per week to work. Consistent with this, the Survey Research Center Study[3] done in 1965 found that employed married women had an average total weekly work time of 69 hours per week compared with a total of 55 hours for wives who did not work. That study also found that working wives made up the difference by sacrificing sleep and passive leisure activities such as reading or watching television.* Nor were working-wife families more likely than homemaker families to purchase labor-saving devices.[4]

With the fall of real wages between 1965 and 1969, and the precipitous drop that began after 1972 and continues to the present time, the logic of the economists' model would seem to suggest that married women ought to substitute home production for market work. But, as is well known, the influx of wives into the labor force has continued apace. Moreover, the corollary to the substitution effect—namely, that married women with young children would generally not find it worthwhile to work—became increasingly difficult to maintain as labor force participation rates for wives with

---

* It should be noted that employed wives did spend less time on housework than wives who were homemakers. However, even women who were employed full time continued to devote an average of 34 hours a week to household tasks.

children under age six increased from 23.3 percent in 1965 to 43.2 percent in 1979 (see Table 1-1). Nevertheless, economists endeavored valiantly to save their theory of female labor supply through an appeal to underlying changes in women's *preferences* for paid activity in the labor market and unpaid work at home. *Ex post* (again), it was abundantly clear to economists that whereas women used to prefer to stay home, raise children, and do housework, attitudes had changed and they now favored paid activities in the labor market. The Supermom phenomenon of the 1970s in which women, if we judge them by their actions, apparently "preferred" to accomplish both (superbly, at that), went unnoted by economists. In light of their reliance on a theory of female labor supply entirely devoid of historical content, it is hardly surprising that economists consistently underestimated the labor supply of women, and married women in particular, in the years following World War II.

Having been burnt in the past by making predictions on the basis of an ahistorical theory, economists now appear ready to atone for past sins by making projections of female labor supply in the 1990s without reference to either history or theory. The accepted methodology encompasses the following steps. First, a projection of the working-age female population is required. This is a relatively easy task since all of the women who will be old enough to work in the 1990s have already been born. Deaths and migration, however, have to be taken into account. Second, the demographic composition—that is, the age-marital-family status groups—of the female population must be specified. One study simply "assumed that, within each age group, the marital and family composition of the female population would remain approximately as it was in 1977."[5] Finally, participation rates within each group have to be projected. This is most often done simply by extrapolating the participation rates within each group from data for the preceding ten or twenty years. The justification for this procedure is occasionally carefully considered. Thus Ralph Smith concludes on the basis of an extensive analysis of the determinants of future labor force growth "that most of the economic, social, and demographic factors that have contributed to the rapid growth in the female labor force in recent years will continue to propel women into the labor market and encourage them to remain there."[6] More often, unfortunately, when projections of female labor supply are made by extrapolating from previous participation rates, "it is *implicitly assumed* that the participation rates of women of childbearing and childrearing age will follow the basic trends which they have exhibited [emphasis added]."[7] The issue for economists, of course, is precisely whether such an assumption can be sustained, whether most of the economic factors that have contributed to the increase in the participation rates of married women can, in fact, be expected to continue to prevail.

The argument that will be developed in the next section suggests that, in fact, the experience of the last ten or twenty years will be a particularly poor guide to understanding what is going to happen in the next ten or twenty. Changes already under way threaten to undermine the position of women in the labor market. While past projections based on economic theory consistently underestimated the growth in employment of married women, there is every reason to believe that current projections derived from extrapolations based on past experience will overestimate their employment growth during the next decade.

An Historical Approach to Employment Trends

Our argument, advanced as well in Chapter 1, is that trends in women's labor force participation cannot be adequately understood using standard economic analysis. The aggregate outcome cannot be interpreted simply as the sum of the individual labor supply decisions made by women and their families. On the contrary, women's participation in production, the nature of the work they perform, and the division of labor between the sexes depends in part on the nature of the production process and on the labor requirements associated with the process of growth during particular periods, as well as on the ability of husbands' wages to adequately support the family unit.[8] Thus, in the decade and a half immediately following World War II, the impetus for the rise in female labor force participation rates came from the growth in stereotypically female service, sales, and clerical occupations. This growth was the result of the expansion of administrative bureaucracies in both the public and private sectors as the scale of public services and private enterprises increased. It also resulted from the growth of the distribution system as production of food products and manufactured goods expanded. Growth in the feminized sectors of the economy occurred just as the pool of single women, who were preferred for these jobs, was declining as a consequence of the "baby-bust" years of the 1930s and the trends toward more years of schooling and earlier age at first marriage. For similar reasons, plus the loss of life during World War II, growth in the pool of male workers just kept pace with the growth of traditionally male jobs. Employers, therefore, turned to the only available population group to fill these jobs—married women; and the women responded. Among married women whose youngest child was in school, the labor force participation rate jumped from 26 percent in 1948 to 43 percent in 1965, edging up to 47 percent in 1979. Their motives in taking jobs when the opportunity arose were probably no different than those of other labor force groups: Employment is a means of upgrading or maintaining skills, of gaining self-respect, and of increasing total family income. The full ramifications of this historically specific growth process, with its rapid increase in employment opportunities for married women, cannot be captured, as economists assume, in the rising real wages of women workers during that period. Without denigrating the effects of rising real wages, it must be noted that the independent effects include the influence of job opportunities on individual work decisions as well as changes in social and employer attitudes toward hiring married women as it became clear that the labor requirements of the growth process then under way could not be met without an influx of wives into the labor force.

In the 1970s declining real wages undermined the ability of men to command an income sufficient, in combination with the unpaid work of their wives at home, to meet family needs. Job opportunities for married women continued to exist even when economic activity slowed down after 1973. In the context of declining real wages, the family of a married woman who left the labor force would suffer an immediate and substantial reduction in real income, with little hope of making it up through increased home production or an increase in the husband's wages. To avoid the decline in family living standards, women worked more continuously and labor force participation rates of young, married women with preschool children increased dramatically.

Labor Force Participation of Married Women in the Next Decade

An historical approach suggests that neither standard economic theory nor simple extrapolation from past data are sufficient to assess the future trend in the labor force participation rate of married women. It is necessary, in addition, to give careful consideration to those factors that condition women's participation in production:

- the nature of the production process;
- the labor requirements associated with economic growth; and
- the adequacy of husbands' earnings.

The Production Process

The most important change in the production process that will affect the employment of women is already well under way: the automation of the office. Computers are already widely used in large enterprises such as corporations, government agencies, public school systems, universities, hospitals, and similar institutions. Their applicability to such clerical functions as the creation, filing, retrieval, copying, moving, and transforming of information is already obvious. Some enterprises are even moving in the direction of keeping and transmitting information electronically, dispensing entirely with paper records and making the "paperless office" a reality. The automated office of the future, in which all typewriters are replaced by computer consoles connected to duplicating devices and capable of simultaneously producing output in machine-readable and human-readable form, promises to revolutionize the traditional clerical function.

It is true, of course, that clerical workers in large organizations, where automation is most likely to be adopted in the next decade, perform a variety of tasks that do not involve the routine processing of paper documents. Nevertheless, one informed observer, an executive at Bell Laboratories, notes that[9]

> *Clerks in such an enterprise do handle a lot of paper. At a rough estimate, perhaps 15 to 20 percent of their time is spent creating records or transcribing them from manuscript to typed or machine-readable form. Perhaps another 15 or 20 percent is devoted to filing, indexing, searching, retrieving, copying, distributing, and delivering records of one sort or another.*

> *The transition to a paperless office will mean that some clerical jobs such as mail distributor and copying machine operator will nearly disappear, as it becomes cheap and easy to recall documents from a computer and display them on a terminal with good resolution and contrast. Other jobs, such as stenographer, will stay recognizably the same but will involve the creation of computer-readable text rather than typed memoranda. And some clerical jobs such as receptionist,*

photographic assistant, and conference registrar, will be affected only
slightly. Overall, one would expect a reduction of the total clerical
effort by perhaps 20 to 30 percent.

While careful studies of the employment impact of the automated office on clerical employment have not been done in the United States, the estimate of a 20 to 30 percent reduction in the clerical labor force required at current output levels is in line with estimates made elsewhere. Thus Siemans, a West German high technology firm, estimates that 40 percent of the work done in offices is suitable for automation by 1990.[10] This would result, according to Siemans, in a 25 to 30 percent reduction in clerical labor requirements.

The short-run outlook for clerical workers, 80 percent of whom are women (see Table 1-3), is that foreseeable changes in information processing within the office will decrease job opportunities in clerical work. Technological unemployment for some office workers is a distinct possibility; and a slowdown in the growth of employment opportunities for clerical workers as routine information processing is automated seems assured.

Economic Growth and Labor Requirements

Office automation is a labor-saving technology. It reduces costs by reducing the labor required to perform a given amount of work. The argument presented in the previous section suggests that in the short run women workers will be displaced or have their opportunities reduced by changes in the production process. Women workers can expect to bear the major cost of introducing a new technology from which society in general expects to benefit. This is a serious problem, but it is not the only issue. The larger question is whether this reduction in job opportunities for women is a transient phenomenon associated with the introduction of the new technology, or whether it can be expected to persist after the initial adjustment period. Will women workers be absorbed in the future by new labor requirements?

There are, in fact, two questions that need to be answered. The first is whether the new technology will result in other job opportunities becoming available; the second is whether such opportunities will be available to women. Economists generally argue that permanent unemployment is not a consequence of increased mechanization or automation. The automated office means that there will be fewer workers per unit of output and fewer workers per unit of capital equipment. But it does not necessarily mean that, after the initial adjustment period, there will be fewer workers in total. As clerical costs are reduced and total labor costs per unit of ouput decline, the prices of those goods and services in which clerical work is an important component will decline (or rise more slowly than income). The income freed up in this process will be spent either to buy more of these goods and services or to buy other products, leading in either case to a growth in demand for total output and to a growth in employment. Thus, to assess the longer run effects of the new technology on women workers, we need some idea of the magnitude of the reduction in costs.

While a reasonable estimate of the reduction in the clerical work force in large enterprises is that it will decline an average of 20 to 30 percent per unit of output, the net saving to these organizations will be much smaller. One writer estimates that[11]

> *even assuming that the hardware cost for a paperless office becomes insignificant compared to the cost of labor (probably a safe assumption), the clerical saving is not a clear gain. It is partially offset by the methods work, the analysis and computer programming, and the planning and replanning required to support mechanization. Thus the net saving to this enterprise from conversion of clerical work to paperless form is unlikely to be more than 15 percent of the current cost of clerical work. This is certainly worthwhile . . . but it's not a revolution.*

Thus the reduction in costs will be about 15 percent of clerical costs while the reduction in employment will be 20 to 30 percent of the clerical work force. Even if, as economists expect, the cost reduction ultimately leads to an overall increase in the demand for output, the rate of growth of job opportunities for clerical workers is not likely to return to its former level. Will the differences be made up through a growth in other job opportunities for women?

Within the institutions in which office work is automated, economic growth implies an increase in opportunities for personnel employed to support the automated offices. Such enterprises will need programmers to design, write, test, and install software, and mechanics to maintain the new office equipment. Additionally, such firms will require highly trained employees capable of analyzing office routine and designing particular computer applications, and skilled in system testing and conversions. These are all typically male occupations. Economic growth may also occur in those sectors of the economy in which clerical work is not an important component of production, for example, construction. These, too, tend to be male-dominated. Thus, whether the female clerical workers made redundant by the new office technology will find employment in the newly expanding occupations depends, ultimately, on an end to sex bias in hiring and the sex labeling of jobs, and on large increases in the employment of women in occupations that are currently predominantly male. The slow pace of progress in this area during the last three decades does not augur well for the future. It is unlikely that slower growth in requirements for clerical workers will be entirely offset by an increase in the proportion of women in stereotypically male jobs. In the absence of a public policy response, the outlook over the next decade is for increasing redundance of part of the female labor force.

An increase in affirmative action programs and a public commitment to integrating women more fully into the labor force and assuring their increased representation in occupations in which they are underrepresented is one approach to this problem. The alternative is a public campaign to return women to their traditional roles within the family. Twice before, in recent American history, the latter approach has been adopted.[12] During the early years of the Depression the view that women were competing with men for jobs and driving up the unemployment rate gained wide acceptance. The response was a conservative backlash embodying traditional ideas about the approriate socioeconomic role for women. Women were returned to homemaking, often involuntarily, by the overall lack of jobs and by socially sanctioned employer discrimination against them in hiring and firing. Again, following the end of World War II, there was widespread fear that depression would accompany demobilization. Somehow, the eleven million men in the armed forces and out of the labor force in 1945 would have to be absorbed. The large number of industrial jobs held by women was viewed as a major impediment to the smooth demobilization of the veterans without massive unemployment. Social pressure for women's return to their traditional roles built up rapidly, and female labor force participation rates declined for several years after 1944.

The view that the emergence of married women from the home and their entrance into the labor force is responsible for many of society's problems is being put forward once again. Slow economic growth during the 1970s has been accompanied by a resurgence of views held during the 1930s. In some quarters, at least, women are seen as exacerbating the economic crisis by competing with men for

jobs. Their presence in the workplace instead of the home is blamed
for a wide variety of real and imagined social ills. Social pressure to
return women to the role of wife, mother, and homemaker is building. The Republican platform on which President Reagan ran in the
1980 election was quite explicit. It said: "We affirm our belief in the
traditional role and value of the family in our society. . . The importance of the support for the mother and homemaker in maintaining
the values of this country cannot be overemphasized." The first steps
toward implementing this platform have already been taken. Wom-
en's control over the timing of pregnancies and, hence, over the
timing and continuity of their employment is threatened by de-
creased funding for sex education and by the Human Life Amendment. The so-called Family Protection Act threatens the non-
traditional family structures in which many women live. The
absence of a policy with respect to day care *de facto* limits employment possibilities for women who want to combine work and family.
Opposition to ERA legislation and withdrawal of support for affirmative action directly affect employment opportunities for women. If
the slow economic growth of the 1970s continues into the 1980s, and
if the growth in employment opportunities in the clerical occupations slows down, social pressure in support of a voluntary or involuntary return by married women to traditional roles is likely to be
mobilized.

Economic Necessity and the Employment of Women

The result of such pressures is not likely to be an actual decline in
the number, or even the proportion, of married women in the labor
force. The relationship of women to paid employment is much less
tenuous than it was in the 1930s or 1940s. Women are firmly planted
in the "feminized" sectors of the economy, and employers have
structured production and distribution to take advantage of their
availability to perform low-paid tasks. Moreover, the current pos-
ture of the U.S. economy suggests that real income gains for American workers will continue to be slow in the 1980s. Cheap energy is
gone for the foreseeable future. The necessity of revamping an
energy-inefficient industrial structure and developing alternative
energy sources—the re-industrialization problems—implies the
slow growth of consumption and of real incomes. As in the 1970s,
economic necessity and the desire to maintain customary standards
of living will act as an impetus to keep many married women in the

labor force. The effect of the campaign to keep married women in traditional roles will be to provide social sanction for ending affirmative action programs and for limiting the penetration of women into the administrative, professional, and craft occupations that are presently the domain of male workers.

Conclusion

The analysis presented in this chapter strongly suggests that we cannot afford to be sanguine about the continued existence of the economic, social, and demographic factors that have contributed in the last thirty years to the steady increase in labor force participation rates of married women. If the labor market becomes increasingly inhospitable to the aspirations of women—if opportunities to move out of female occupations occur more slowly and the growth in clerical positions is less rapid than expected—the growth in labor force participation rates for married women can also be expected to slow. This is especially true in light of the resurgence of support for traditional sex roles within the family.

Forecasts about the growth in labor force participation rates—one study projects that the participation rate for married woman will increase from 55.5 percent in March 1978 to 66.7 percent in 1990[13]—appear overly optimistic. Such forecasts are based on the belief that labor market opportunities for married women will improve as rapidly in the future as they have in the past, that women will be able to move more easily into male occupations, and that younger women today have more liberal attitudes toward the employment of married women. Neither opportunities nor attitudes are fixed, however, and recent experience may not prove accurate as an indicator of future trends in the participation of women in production.

Endnotes

1. Ralph E. Smith, "The Movement of Women into the Labor Force" in Ralph E. Smith, ed., *The Subtle Revolution: Women at Work* (Washington, D.C.: The Urban Institute, 1979), p. 5. Similar arguments have been advanced by other economists. See, for example, Glen Cain, *Married Women in the Labor Force: An Economic Analysis* (Chicago: University of Chicago Press, 1966), and Jacob Mincer, "Labor Force Participation of Married Women: A Study of Labor

Supply" in *Aspects of Labor Economics* (Princeton, N.J.: Princeton University Press, 1962).

2. Kathryn E. Walker and Margaret E. Woods, *Time Use: A Measure of Household Production of Family Goods and Services* (American Home Economics Association, 1976). Cited in Clair Vickery, "Women's Economic Contribution to the Family" in Ralph E. Smith, ed., *The Subtle Revolution: Women at Work* (Washington, D.C.: The Urban Institute, 1979).

3. Survey Research Center, "Summary of the United States Time Use Survey," University of Michigan, Institute for Social Research, 1966.

4. Myra H. Strober and Charles B. Weinberg, "Working Wives and Major Family Expenditures," *Journal of Consumer Research*, 2–3 (December 1977), pp. 141–147.

5. Smith, *op. cit.*, p. 16.

6. *Ibid.*, p. 17.

7. Howard N. Fullerton, Jr. and Paul O. Flaim, *New Labor Force Projections to 1990*, Special Labor Force Report No. 197. Reprinted from December 1976 *Monthly Labor Review*.

8. This approach was suggested at least in part by an article by Lourdes Beneria, "Reproduction, Production and the Sexual Division of Labor," *Cambridge Journal of Economics*, 3 (1979), pp. 203–225.

9. Victor A. Vyssotsky, "The Use of Computers for Business Functions" in Michael L. Dertouzos and Joel Moses, eds., *The Computer Age: A Twenty Year View* (Cambridge, Mass.: MIT Press, 1979), p. 132. Reprinted by permission of the MIT Press.

10. "The Job-Killers of Germany," *New Scientist* (June 8, 1978).

11. Vyssotsky, *op. cit.*, pp. 132–133.

12. For a fuller discussion, particularly with reference to the 1930s, see Jane Humphries, "Women: Scapegoats and Safety Valves in the Great Depression," *The Review of Radical Political Economics*, 8 (Spring 1976), pp. 56–68.

13. Ralph E. Smith, *Women in the Labor Force in 1990*, cited in Smith, *op. cit.*, Table 1, pp. 14–15.

APPENDIX

Appendix Tables A-1, A-2, and A-3 report the means and coefficients of the wage equations in 1972 and 1976. This is the underlying information used in computing Table 3-2. Appendix Tables A-4 and A-5 report mean values for selected personal, family, and work experience characteristics for married women, husband present, in 1972.

Table A-1 Means and Coefficients of the 1972 Wage Equations for White Women Employed in 1972 (t-statistics in parentheses)

Variable	Gap ≥ 3		Gap < 3	
	Mean $(\bar{X}_d D)$	Coefficient (f_d)	Mean $(\bar{X}_t C)$	Coefficient (f_c)
Late 30s in 1972[a]	0.221	11.570 (0.962)	0.345	27.876 (1.861)
Late 40s in 1972	0.469	12.917 (1.237)	0.321	11.498 (0.456)
Good health	0.891	23.405 (1.696)	0.901	−35.013 (−1.723)
Years of schooling	11.675	7.415 (2.862)	11.952	12.473 (3.543)
Father has 10 or more years of schooling	0.253	25.518 (2.520)	0.242	20.161 (1.392)
Husband present	0.835	0.081 (0.007)	0.818	−1.599 (−0.102)
Child under 6 years of age at home	0.053	23.787 (1.010)	0.119	46.434 (1.737)
Child 6–17 years of age at home	0.824	−2.012 (−0.148)	0.754	3.156 (0.164)
Years worked 6 months or more through 1967	8.507	1.710 (1.867)	12.444	2.586 (2.314)
Weeks worked 1968–1972	167.691	0.213 (2.194)	173.175	0.371 (2.515)
Works full time (35 hours or more)	0.693	3.314 (0.327)	0.754	33.999 (2.158)
Tenure on current job	4.664	2.390 (1.868)	5.631	4.589 (3.392)

Table A-1 (continued)

Variable	Gap ≥ 3		Gap < 3	
	Mean ($\bar{X}_iD$)	Coefficient (f_a)	Mean ($\bar{X}_iC$)	Coefficient (f_c)
Job covered by union contract	0.200	44.761	0.163	81.530
		(4.037)		(4.981)
Resides in South	0.227	-15.865	0.242	-1.427
		(-1.479)		(-0.101)
Local labor force numbers less than 400,000	0.664	-32.707	0.746	-52.158
		(-3.476)		(-3.719)
Professional, technical, or managerial occupations[b]	0.163	58.652	0.254	73.904
		(4.329)		(4.518)
Other occupations	0.387	-32.943	0.341	-48.210
		(-2.952)		(-3.027)
Manufacturing, mining, construction, or agriculture industries[c]	0.269	50.332	0.230	34.719
		(3.834)		(1.820)
Professional services	0.323	34.420	0.337	14.737
		(2.684)		(0.785)
Other services	0.043	25.552	0.052	-2.620
		(11.106)		(-0.910)
Public administration, public utilities, finance, insurance, and real estate	0.171	55.910	0.198	45.299
		(3.704)		(2.300)
Constant		73.110		18.503
		(1.791)		(0.757)
Mean value of 1972 wages	274.7		306.9	
N		375		252
R^2		0.414		0.579
F		11.855		15.040

[a] Reference category: Early 40s in 1972.   [b] Reference category: Clerical occupations.   [c] Reference category: Wholesale and retail trade.

Table A-2 Means and Coefficients of the 1976 Wage Equations for White Women Employed in 1976 (t-statistics in parentheses)

Variable	Gap $\geq$ 3		Gap $<$ 3	
	Mean ($\bar{X}_i D$)	Coefficient (f_d)	Mean ($\bar{X}_i C$)	Coefficient (f_c)
Early 40s in 1976[a]	0.259	4.910	0.336	20.265
		(0.349)		(0.834)
Early 50s in 1976	0.420	1.417	0.304	10.583
		(0.108)		(0.408)
Good health	0.877	1.070	0.895	16.644
		(0.064)		(0.484)
Years of schooling	11.759	7.022	11.972	13.345
		(2.331)		(2.111)
Father has 10 or more years of schooling	0.254	31.461	0.259	11.576
		(2.485)		(0.472)
Husband present	0.804	12.823	0.810	-29.865
		(0.942)		(-1.142)
Child under 18 years of age at home	0.768	-0.202	0.802	-41.377
		(-0.015)		(-1.505)
Years worked 6 or more months through 1967	7.944	2.729	11.972	1.613
		(2.392)		(0.862)
Weeks worked 1968–1972	136.010	0.134	152.777	0.651
		(1.608)		(3.375)
Weeks worked 1974	38.932	0.823	41.211	0.425
		(2.410)		(0.533)
Weeks worked 1976	41.640	1.294	41.154	0.980
		(3.474)		(1.430)
Works full time (35 hours or more)	0.679	34.204	0.713	-3.799
		(2.735)		(-0.144)

Table A-2 (continued)

Variable	Gap ≥ 3		Gap < 3	
	Mean ($\bar{X}_iD$)	Coefficient (f_d)	Mean ($\bar{X}_iC$)	Coefficient (f_c)
Resides in South	0.232	-39.708 (-3.055)	0.235	14.785 (0.614)
Local labor force numbers less than 400,000	0.669	-36.978 (-3.183)	0.725	-66.759 (-2.841)
Professional, technical or managerial occupations[b]	0.162	81.058 (4.897)	0.271	93.145 (3.359)
Other occupations	0.413	-25.387 (-1.934)	0.364	-50.103 (-1.864)
Manufacturing, mining, construction, or agriculture industries[c]	0.225	76.160 (4.653)	0.190	63.689 (1.900)
Professional services	0.331	57.616 (3.772)	0.312	42.268 (1.305)
Other services	0.065	-0.388 (0.016)	0.081	-22.028 (-0.519)
Public administration, public utilities, finance, insurance, or real estate	0.167	96.171 (5.176)	0.215	79.170 (2.474)
Constant		73.544 (1.574)		103.887 (1.074)
Mean value of 1976 wages	347.0		410.7	
N		414		247
R^2		0.443		0.423
F		15.605		8.273

[a] Reference category: Late 40s in 1976.
[b] Reference category: Clerical occupations.
[c] Reference category: Wholesale and retail trade.

Table A-3 Means and Coefficients of the 1976 Wage Equations for White Women Employed in Both 1972 and 1976 (t-statistics in parentheses)

	Gap $\geq$ 3		Gap $<$ 3	
Variable	*Mean ($\bar{X}_iD$)*	*Coefficient (f_a)*	*Mean ($\bar{X}_iC$)*	*Coefficient (f_c)*
Early 40s in 1976[a]	0.218	20.330 (1.127)	0.323	27.414 (0.958)
Early 50s in 1976	0.462	-1.586 (-0.101)	0.304	11.705 (0.386)
Good health	0.875	0.689 (0.034)	0.906	16.050 (0.367)
Years of schooling	11.683	8.099 (2.179)	12.090	14.636 (1.949)
Father has 10 or more years of schooling	0.260	36.942 (2.432)	0.264	17.365 (0.604)
Husband present	0.811	20.277 (1.187)	0.791	-33.053 (-1.085)
Child under 18 years of age at home	0.737	-8.048 (-0.502)	0.776	-53.899 (-1.748)
Years worked 6 or more months through 1967	8.641	3.144 (2.308)	12.279	0.761 (0.336)
Weeks worked 1968–1972	166.321	0.104 (0.736)	175.552	0.749 (2.549)
Weeks worked 1974	44.186	1.152 (2.316)	45.930	0.863 (0.763)
Weeks worked 1976	43.205	1.452 (2.881)	43.940	0.493 (0.558)
Works full time (35 hours or more)	0.734	43.790 (2.651)	0.776	-21.280 (-0.643)

Table A-3 (continued)

Variable	Gap ≥ 3		Gap < 3	
	Mean ($\bar{X}$,D)	Coefficient (f_a)	Mean ($\bar{X}$,C)	Coefficient (f_c)
Resides in South	0.247	-47.714 (-3.015)	0.234	12.792 (0.444)
Local labor force numbers less than 400,000	0.647	-39.138 (-2.762)	0.761	-81.801 (-2.903)
Professional, technical, or managerial occupations[b]	0.173	91.329 (4.710)	0.318	85.127 (2.745)
Other occupations	0.381	-26.289 (-1.626)	0.304	-77.907 (-2.432)
Manufacturing, mining, construction, or agriculture industries[c]	0.244	78.258 (3.861)	0.194	78.011 (1.933)
Professional services	0.359	57.744 (3.031)	0.348	49.577 (1.312)
Other services	0.045	11.746 (0.337)	0.065	-21.251 (-0.643)
Public administration, public utilities, finance, insurance, or real estate	0.170	106.117 (4.503)	0.204	97.831 (2.506)
Constant		30.703 (0.528)		119.017 (1.004)
Mean value of 1976 wages	367.0		440.2	
N		312		201
R^2		0.443		0.394
F		11.560		5.842

[a] Reference category: Late 40s in 1976.
[b] Reference category: Clerical occupations.
[c] Reference category: Wholesale and retail trade.

Table A-4   Profile of Selected Personal and Family Characteristics, 1972

	Mothers, Husbands Present	
Characteristics	*Gap $\geq$ 3*	*Gap $<$ 3*
Proportion whose father's education $\geq$ 10	24.5%	26.3%
Average number of years of schooling	11.6 years	11.9 years
Proportion who are in their late 30s	22.6%	36.4%
Proportion who are in their early 40s	31.2%	36.8%
Proportion who are in their late 40s	46.2%	26.8%
Proportion who are in good health	90.3%	89.9%
Proportion who have child $<$ 6 years old	4.1%	14.7%
Proportion who have child 6–17 years old	85.2%	73.2%
Proportion with no children at home 17 or younger	10.7%	12.1%
Husband's average annual earnings	$ 9,039	$10,102
Proportion in areas where the local labor force numbers 300,000 or less	62.9%	68.2%

Table A-5   Mean Values of Selected Work Experience Characteristics, 1972

	Mothers, Husbands Present	
Characteristics	*Gap $\geq$ 3*	*Gap $<$ 3*
Number of years worked 6 or more months by 1967	8.4 years	12.2 years
Number of weeks worked between 1968 and 1972	167 weeks	171 weeks
Tenure on current job (years)	4.6 years	5.8 years
Proportion who have jobs that are covered by union contract	21.7%	17.7%
Proportion who work full time, 35 hours or more	68.2%	72.2%
Hourly earnings	$2.77	$3.10
Social status of the job (Bose index)	47.5	49.7

INDEX